Contemporary Piano Method book 4

by Margaret Brandman

Exclusive distributors for Australia and New Zealand
Encore Music Distributors
227 Napier St, Fitzroy VIC 3065 Australia
Phone +61 3 9415 6677
Facsimile +61 3 9415 6655
Email sales@encoremusic.com.au

This book © Copyright 2018 by Margaret Brandman trading as Jazzem Music
46 Gerrale St, Cronulla NSW 2230 Australia
ISBN 978-0-949683-28-1
ORDER NUMBER MMP 8027
International copyright secured (APRA/AMCOS). All rights reserved.

Unauthorised reproduction of any part of this publication by any means,
including photocopying, is an infringement of copyright.

CONTEMPORARY PIANO METHOD - BOOK 4

INTRODUCTION

This method is designed to equip the student with the necessary skills to play both Classical and Modern music, including Popular and Jazz styles, with ease and understanding while giving experience in skills required for both classical and contemporary examination syllabi. The piano method is the central core of an integrated course which provides materials for ear training (audio and workbooks), theory, technique, improvisation and repertoire pieces in all styles.

The methodology incorporates various learning styles or modalities, including:

* aural training
* spatial reasoning -visual, aural and tactile
* colour - to impart the meanings of the duration of the notes
* visualisation and the use of pictorial representations of the intervals
* the gestalt approach to topics (the whole view)
* knowledge of keyboard geography
* shape and pattern reading
* harmonic analysis
* improvisation
* transposition

Following on from book 3 in the series, Book 4 continues :

The streamlined interval approach to reading.
This is achieved when the aural, tactile and visual aspects of music are combined so that students are able to read and play by following the flow of intervals. Level Four continues the development of music speed-reading and learning skills to a high degree by applying the skill to reading complex chords.

Rhythm
This book expands students horizons by exploring ways in which compositions can be written to express freedom in rhythm.

Keyboard Geography
The keyboard pattern approach is used to teach diminished and whole-tone scales.

Understanding Harmonic Structure and Modulation
A unique feature of this course is that it requires students to be actively engaged in the task of discovering the underlying harmonic structure of music, using the information to speed up the learning process, build an aural awareness of keys and chords, and to use as a basis for improvisation.

This book continues the exploration of harmonies established in the earlier books in this series, and extends the harmonic palette to include alterations in the extended chords.

Keyboard Harmony and Improvisation
The knowledge of the sounds of various scales and chords and modes and their keyboard patterns is fostered so that they may be used as tools for improvisation. In this book the topic of Root Progressions, introduced in Book 3, is continued through to Step 8. . Students are shown how arrange pieces by supplying substitute chords to a progression. The book also continues to develop students' ability to play from printed chord symbols as well as being able to realize a figured bass.

Styles of Music

This book, presents many pieces which demonstrate compositional devices and piano techniques of the Twentieth Century and beyond. The topic of polyphonic composition is taken to the advanced level with the inclusion of Bach's Prelude and Fugue. The range of styles gives the student skills to become both a professional musician in the popular field, and a competent and informed performer of classical and contemporary music. Parallels are drawn between the harmonic devices of the classical and modern composers.

To fully understand the theoretical concepts in this book, students are advised to work through the accompanying theory and aural texts and audio which are listed below.

I trust that the student will enjoy working through the method and will gain an appreciation of the variety of music and also the inter-relationship between music of different ages, countries and periods. It is my belief, as demonstrated with my own students over many years, that through the understanding of the workings of each piece, the study process is made easier and more interesting, the appreciation of sounds increases and the resulting performance of each piece is more meaningful to both performer and listener.

For more detailed information on the ideas and information in the series refer to my web site:

www.margaretbrandman.com

Margaret Brandman (Dr)
Ph.D (Mus/Arts) B.Mus., T.Mus.A
F.Comp.ASMC.,F.Mus.Ed.ASMCL.Perf.ASMC
Hon.FNMSM., A.Mus.A., ASA T.Dip.

INTEGRATED SUPPORT MATERIALS FOR THIS LEVEL
* Pictorial Patterns for Keyboard Scales and Chords
* Its Easy to Improvise
* Dreamweaving
* Twelve Timely Pieces
* Contemporary Modal Pieces
* Blues and Boogie-Woogie
* Six Contemporary Pieces
* Reflections - concert work for piano
* Sonorities - concert work for piano
* Static Ripples - Piano Duet

THEORY/AURAL
* Contemporary Aural Course - Sets 4 to 6
* Contemporary Aural Course – Set 7 Hear Your Chords!
* Contemporary Aural Course – Set 8 Hear More Chords!
* Contemporary Theory Workbooks 1 and 2
* Contemporary Chord Workbooks 1 and 2
* Harmony Comes Together Book 1

CONTEMPORARY PIANO METHOD
BOOK FOUR
CONTENTS

Music from the Twentieth Century onwards 7

Musical Sound Sources (1) Noise (2) Effects.. 8

No. 1 Flamenco Fantasy, Brandman... 9

ROOT PROGRESSIONS **Step Four** Progression by 2nd or 7ths..........................10

No. 2 Gymnopedie No. 1 by E. Satie... 11

ROOT PROGRESSIONS **Step Five** Progression by 3rds or 6ths......................... 15

Musical Sound Sources (3) Melody.. 16

No. 3 Mystery Movie Mood Music, Brandman.. 17

ROOT PROGRESSIONS **Step Six** Progression by 4ths...................................... 18

Extended Chords (4) Added Notes...19

No. 4 Grape Escape, Brandman... 21

ROOT PROGRESSIONS **Step Seven** Altered Cycle Progressions...................... 22

Application of Step Seven..24

No. 5 Etude No. 2 by F. Chopin.. 25

Figured Bass Exercises. Section Five

    Seventh chords in 2nd and 3rd inversions. The Diminished 7th.........................28

Musical Sound Sources (4) Harmony...29

No. 6 Bells Across the Water, Brandman... 30

Figured Bass Exercises. Section Six. (a) Sus 4 and Sus 9 chords

    (b) Modulation.. 32

No. 7 Three Part Invention No. XI by J. S. Bach...33

ROOT PROGRESSIONS **Step Eight** Equal Divisions of the Octave.................. 36

No. 8 Danses de Travers No.1 by E. Satie.. 38

Musical Sound Sources (5) Rhythm (6) Notation..40

No. 9 Whole-in-One, Brandman. The Whole-Tone Scale...42

Scales in 3rds, 6th and 10ths..44

Chromatic Progressions. Some Effective Chromatic Progressions..45

The Well-Tempered Clavier..48

FUGUE..49

No. 10 Prelude and Fugue No. IX by J. S.Bach..50

The Diminished Scale...54

Figured Bass Exercises. Section Seven
   Playing from Bass line and Figurings only. Further Technique Development......................57

Extended Chords (5) Altered Notes (a) Alterations to the Foundation Notes.......................58

Serial Music..60

No. 11 Write your own piece...61

Extended Chords (6) Altered Notes (a) Alterations to the upper extension notes..................62

Extended Chords (7) Voicing Chords in Fourths (Quartal Harmony)...................................65

No. 12 Waltzing Matilda (Traditional) arranged by M. S. Brandman...................................68

Extended Chords (8) Altered Notes in combination..70

No. 13 Panchromatic Ponderings, Brandman..71

No. 14 First Star At Twilight, Brandman...72

Commonly Used Jazz Scales..78

Polytonality and Polychords...80

No. 15 Polynesian Polypus, Brandman..81

Scales outside the European Classical Tradition..82

No. 16 A Whole World of Sound, Brandman..83

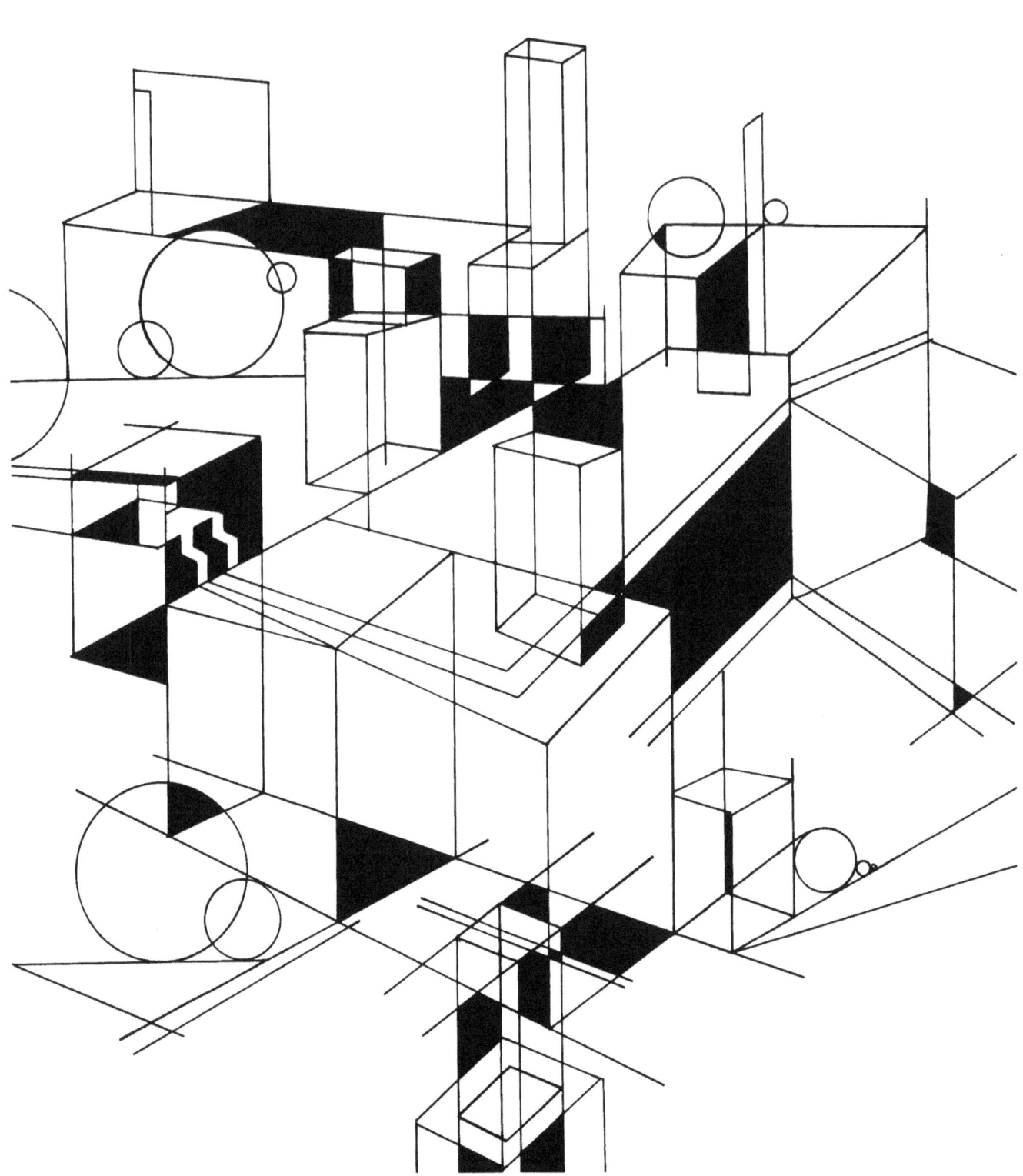

MUSIC IN THE TWENTIETH CENTURY

In Book 3 of this series, the historical development of Modes and their gradual replacement by the Major-Minor system in the 18th Century, was discussed.

The Major-Minor system was explored by composers for approximately one and a half centuries from 1750 to the late 1800's. In the latter part of the 19th Century, chromatic alterations to the key became increasingly prevalent until such time that it was felt that all avenues of the existing system had been fully explored.

Thus it became time to reappraise the 12 Chromatic notes of the scale and find different ways of using them. One of the ways, was to use the notes in a Tone Row with specific rules as to how the notes should be used. This system is known as 'Serial' composition and was first devised by Arnold Schoenberg. See page 60 in this book for more details. Another method was the system of Equal Divisions of the Octave and mirror image rhythms devised by Joseph Shillinger. See page 36.

Other composers, for example Claude Debussy and Erik Satie in France and Dmitri Kabalevsky in Russia and Bela Bartok in Hungary, explored Modal sounds, and Exotic scale sounds. See page 82.

Other aspects of music that were treated in a new way were: Noise (which had not been used at all prior to 1900 except as effects for operas); Melody; Harmony; Rhythm; Notation. Each of these areas will be treated separately on the following pages.

MUSICAL SOUND SOURCES

1. Noise

In the Twentieth Century, noise has become one of the composer's resources. On a keyboard instrument noise can be created in several ways; by knocking or tapping on the wooden or metal parts of the instrument, by using clusters of notes at the extreme ends of the keyboard, and so on.

2. Effects

By using the strings of the piano in a different way, other effects can be gained. The strings can be plucked by hand or brushed by the hand to produce harp effects. A piano can also be 'Prepared', that is; fitted with pieces of cardboard or metal strips on the composers instructions, so that the sound the hammer makes on the strings is altered. A keyboard treated like this can sound like a Honkey-Tonk piano or similar to a harpsichord. Music for an instrument that has been treated in the above manner, is therefore known as music for "Prepared Piano". The natural percussiveness of the keyboard may be highlighted by the use of many accented notes or repetitive patterns on selected notes and the pedal may be used to achieve various harmonic effects rather than in the traditional sense of sustaining chords in a progression.

The following piece employs some of these effects. Look for these devices in other Contemporary pieces.

FLAMENCO FANTASY

The Phrygian Mode and the strumming effects lend to the piece the sound of the Spanish Flamenco guitar and the wood taps are reminiscent of the tapping heels of the Flamenco dancer or the taps that the Flamenco guitarist makes on the body of the guitar during his performance.

IMPROVISATION

Once you have learned the Flamenco Fantasy, improvise a piece of your own using the Phrygian Mode on whatever starting note you wish, and employing some of the melodic devices suggested in the piece, or some of your own choosing.

Write out the Phrygian Mode you have chosen for your improvised piece on the manuscript below.

1. FLAMENCO FANTASY

Margaret S. Brandman

Key: 𝆪 = tap knuckles on open piano lid.

ROOT PROGRESSIONS STEP IV

The first three Steps in the series of Root Progressions that have been presented were based on the CYCLE OF FIFTHS and the use of the LEADING FUNCTION chords. (Dom 7th, Dim 7th and bII7ths).

Any progression based on the Cycle of Fifths will have a very solid feeling to it. National Anthems and marching tunes tend to use these types of progressions, particularly Step 1. (The first few bars of God Save the Queen or God Save America depending on which country you prefer, uses the progression G, Emi, D7, G. So do hundreds of Rock Tunes, Elvis Presley's 'Return to Sender', to name one.)

For such tunes as ballads and less stirring types of tunes, the Root Progressions move in less harmonically solid intervals. The first of these is the ascending or descending SECOND interval. When inverted they also become descending or ascending SEVENTHS. (See Example 1).

In many tunes a series of linking chords can be built on a progression moving in seconds. For instance if the original progression is two bars of C Major moving to a bar of F they could be linked by chords built on a D and an E. (These would substitute for the C Chord in the second bar.) The Progression would then move: C / / /. Dm / Em /. F / / /. The type of chord placed on the Root Notes (in this case minor chords) are found in the Chord Table for that key. (See Example 2).

Depending on the tune in question, you may prefer to use a Progression moving in Seconds rather than one based on the Cycle of Fifths. Once again experiment to see if you would prefer to place a different chord Quality above the Root Note than that found in the Table of Chords.

Example 3, is a Progression in Descending seconds.

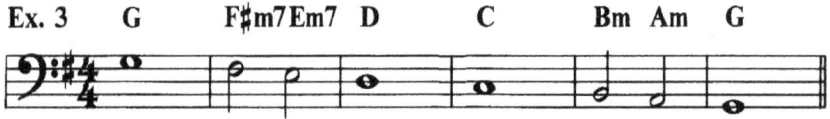

Example 4 is a Twelve Bar Blues which uses a mixture of Steps 1, II, III and IV as substitute chords.

Two tunes which use the ascending second progression are 'Downtown' and 'Here There and Everywhere'. (See Example 5) and the Tune 'Hit the Road Jack' uses the descending 2nd progression in a minor key. (See Example 6).

GYMNOPEDIE NO. 1

by Erik Satie

The following piece is probably Erik Satie's best known piece. It is a favourite subject for improvisation or arrangement by Jazz players, owing to the beautiful modal sounds and unusual movement through various modes.

Even though the Key Signature of two sharps would seem to suggest a key of D Major the first chord (Gmaj7) influences the tonality and lends a Lydian sound to the melody., G Lydian -F♯ and C♯.

The change of mode in bar 21 suggests D Dorian mode while the five bars at the end which are underpinned with an E pedal note have a Phrygian sound to them. The final cadence is in the Dorian mode and produces a 'not quite finished' effect.

ERIK SATIE

I would strongly urge the student to read a biography of this composer. You will discover some interesting facts about this eccentric composer who lived an unusual life and wrote some of the most creative music of the Nineteenth century. His ideas were well ahead of his time which is why he is only just being recognised for the genius that he was, over 50 years after his death.

Suggested further studies

Erik Satie Piano Album published by Cramer, Editor Maurice Rogers.

2. GYMNOPEDIE No. 1

Erik Satie

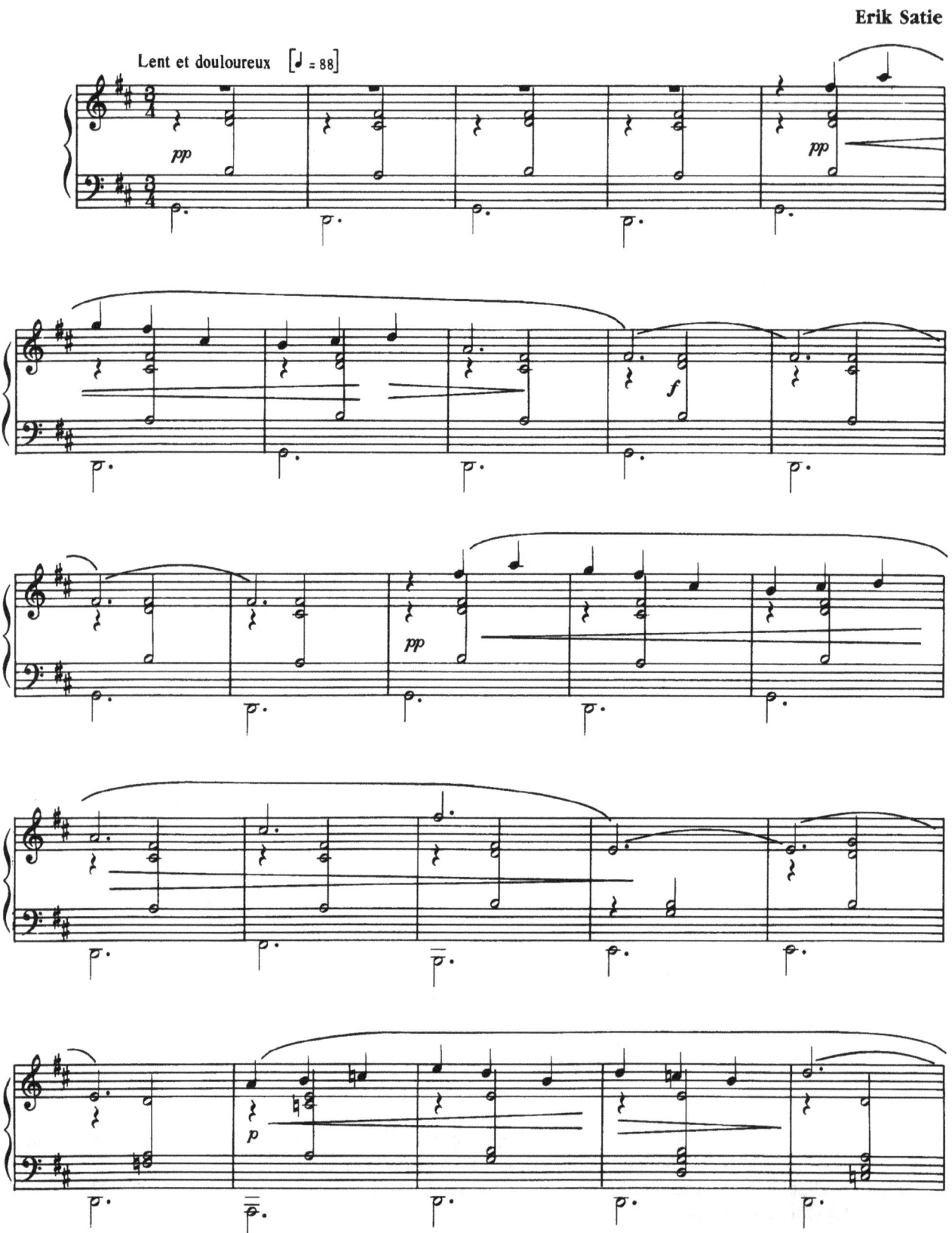

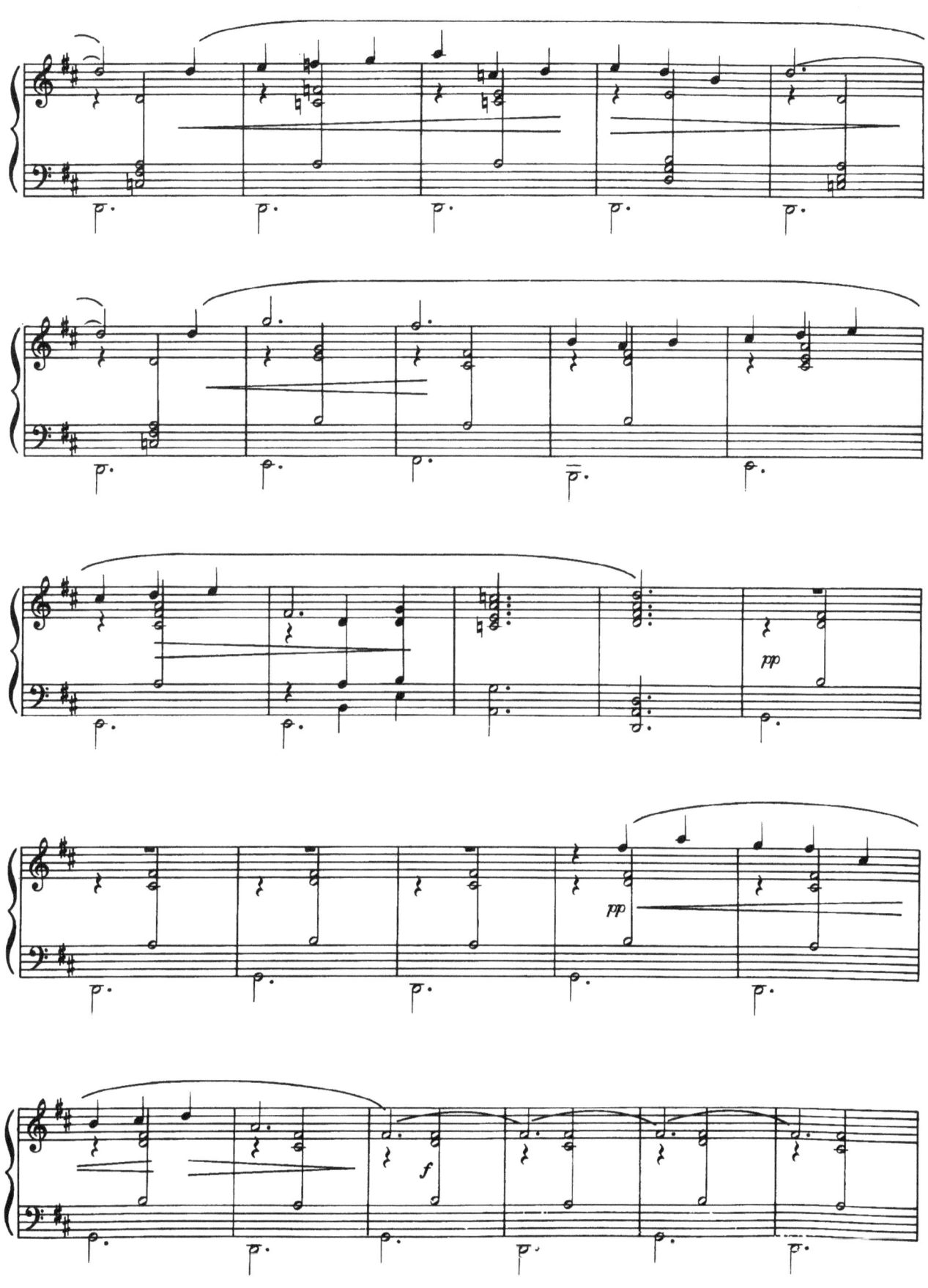

ROOT PROGRESSIONS STEP V

To the four steps in the series on Root Progressions already covered, we can now add Step V which is a Root Progression moving in ascending or descending thirds; when inverted they become ascending or descending 6ths.

Ex. 1

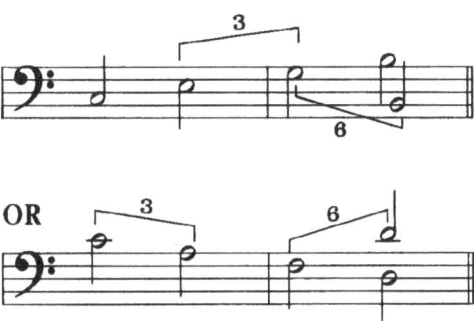

This progression is weaker than the progression in 2nds as most of the notes in the successive chords are the same. Because of this there is not a great feeling of movement, which is why the progression is weak.

However the progression does have its uses. If you want basically the same sound over several bars, but at the same time introducing slight variations, use this progression in thirds.

For example if you built a chord progression in C Major on the Root Notes of C, E, G and B taking each chord from the Major Chord Table, the chords will be C Major, E min, G Major and B diminished. Compare the notes from each chord to the next and notice how many notes they have in common. See Example 2.

Ex. 2

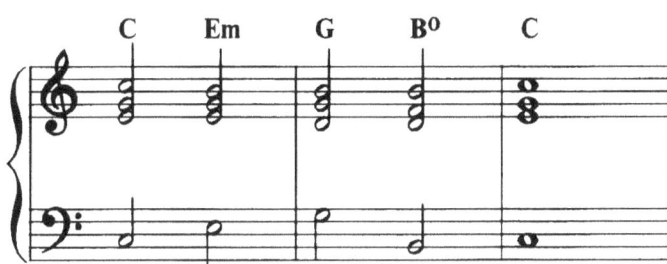

The weaker progressions such as Step IV and Step V will be found more in ballad tunes than in stirring National Anthems or Blues tunes. Try to be aware of the Root Progressions in the pieces you play. Notice the effect each one has. Store this information for the time that you want to write your own tunes or play an improvised piece.

Another way the Root Progression in thirds can be treated is to place all Major Chords above the Root Notes, or all Minor Chords. The contemporary serious composers often used these devices to create different sounds. Experiment to see which sounds you like, placed above a Root Progression in thirds. See Example 3.

Ex. 3

Example 4 is a 12-Bar Blues using a mixture of Steps I–V. Use this example as both a chord study and a vehicle for Right Hand improvisation over Left Hand chords. Use the modes which suit the chords or the Blues scale to create your melodic line.

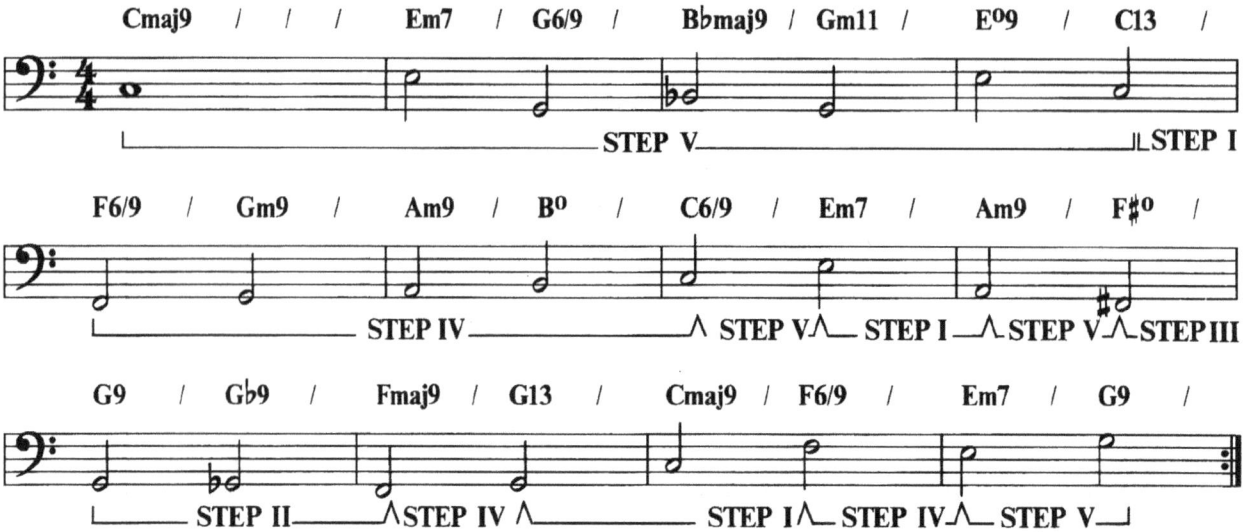

MUSICAL SOUND SOURCES continued.

3. Melody

Music in the 20th Century has departed from the traditional use of melody. The extreme registers of the keyboard are brought into play and melodies move in a jagged manner. The lines may be unpredictable or irregular or procede according to the rules of *Serial composition. To provide more contrast with the music of the previous centuries, the dissonant intervals of Minor Second, Major Seventh, Minor Ninth, Augmented Fourth and so on, are often featured.

The following piece uses some of these features.

*Serial Composition — see page 60.

MYSTERY MOVIE MOOD MUSIC

This piece is written in the Mixolydian mode and uses changing time signatures as well as abrupt accents to create the mood.

Think of your favourite Alfred Hitchcock suspense thriller and the type of music you would hear behind the dramatic moments. The suspense is not relieved in this piece as the Mixolydian mode cannot resolve — just keep your audience dangling!

IMPROVISATION

Using the Mixolydian mode, or another of your own choosing, improvise a piece employing some of the Melodic devices suggested above.

3. MYSTERY MOVIE MOOD MUSIC

Margaret S. Brandman

ROOT PROGRESSIONS STEP VI

This Root Progression is the last of the four progressions that are based on simple interval movement. In Step VI the Root Note moves by intervals of falling 4ths (same as rising 5ths.) It has the opposite effect to the Cycle of 5ths progression which is Step I of this series. (Moving in falling 5ths.)

Whereas a Progression which moves in falling 5ths sounds as if it is establishing a continuous resolving succession of chords, a progression which moves in falling 4ths (i.e. Step VI) sounds as if it is continually climbing, and is therefore used to create a build in tension in special cases where this effect is desired. See Example 1.

To summarise the Root Progressions so far discussed in this book, the first three Steps dealt with basic Cycle Progressions and the substitution of Leading Function chords, and the next three Steps in the series dealt with alternate progressions based on various intervallic movements.

Thus:—

STEP I— The Cycle of Fifths Progression. (Intervals of falling 5ths/rising 4ths).

STEP II— Use of the seventh chord built on the Flattened Second (♭II) as a substitute for the Dominant Seventh Chord. (TRITONE SUBSTITUTION).

STEP III— Use of the chords built on the Seventh Degree of the Major and Minor scale as substitutes for the Dominant Seventh Chord i.e. Diminished triad, or Diminished Seventh or the Half-Diminished Seventh chord. (mi7♭5).

STEP IV— Root Progression moving in ascending or descending 2nds or 7ths.

STEP V— Root Progressions moving in ascending or descending 3rds or 6ths.

STEP VI— Root Progressions moving in descending 4ths (ascending 5ths).

The following Blues Pattern uses all the Root Progressions so far discussed. Play the progression in these two styles:

(1) As written with the single note in the Left Hand and the remainder of the chord in the Right Hand part. Use extension notes to the basic four-note chord indicated, writing in the extensions you have chosen on the chord symbols.

(2) Play the extended chords in the Left Hand omitting the appropriate notes. Add the occasional Root note to the chord in the lower register of the piano connecting the sounds by use of the sustain pedal. Meanwhile improvise a Right Hand melody using the modes as the basis for your improvised lines.

USING THE NINTH, ELEVENTH AND THIRTEENTH NOTES AS ADDED NOTES

Occasionally a composer or player may wish to add just the 13th note to a seventh chord, without the support of the 9th and 11th degrees. The 13th note is then marked in brackets or the word 'add' is written in front of it. Thus C7(13) or C7add13.

The same system can be used for the 11th degree that is used without the support of the 9th, and the 9th degree that is used without support of the 7th. For example:— C7(11) or C7add11; and Cadd9.

THE 'Add 9' CHORD (Also known as a Suspended Ninth chord)

This chord may be either a Major or Minor triad with an added 9th note. As the 9th degree is also known as a Compound 2nd it is sometimes written as an 'add 2' chord. Many players play this chord with the 9th degree placed close to the 3rd degree in a cluster formation while playing the Root Note down one octave.

Thus:

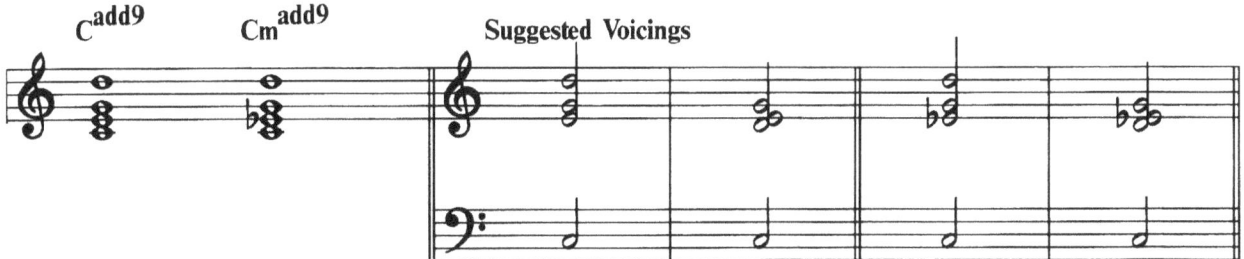

Refer to the Figured Bass exercises, Section 6 on page 32.

THE DOMINANT 7 ADD 13 CHORD

This chord is the Thirteenth Chord found in most Classical Harmony tutors. It is usually written as a four-note chord with the 5th degree omitted. It is also found in popular music as a three-note chord shape. The Root Note is played in the lower register of a keyboard instrument while the remaining three notes (5th omitted entirely) can be spaced a fourth apart, which lends an open sound to the chord. (See page 65).

For Example:—

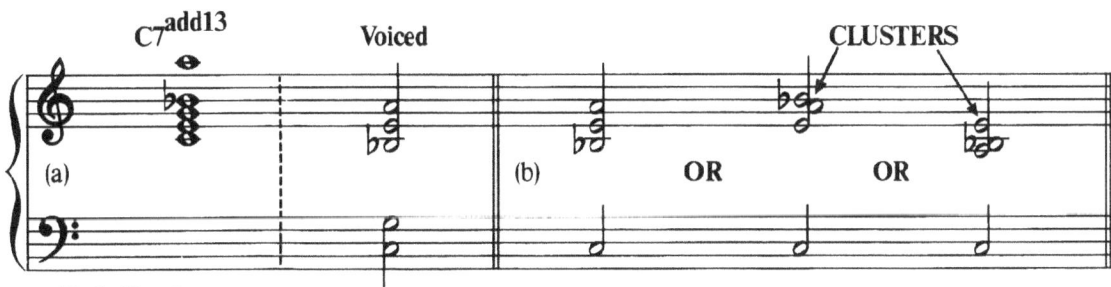

(a) Full Chord
(b) Fifth Omitted

THE DOMINANT 9TH ADD 13 CHORD

This is the more frequently used version of the Dominant 13th sound. It is found in many Jazz and popular tunes. Owing to the fact that the 11th degree is not present, the problems created by the 11th clashing with the 3rd degree of the chord are avoided. **In many publications the chord symbol 13 is intended to imply 9(13).**

To help you decide which form of the 13th chord to play, remember that the 11th degree lends to the sound the feeling of the Amen Cadence. (IV to I). Thus the full Dom 13th sound is popular in much Gospel music and in a great deal of Rock music that has its heritage in Classical music. It has a stronger leading tendancy than the 9(13) chord because of the 11th degree.

In Jazz compositions therefore, the 9(13) chord is used more frequently due to the fact that it can be more readily used as a passing chord that does not require immediate resolution.

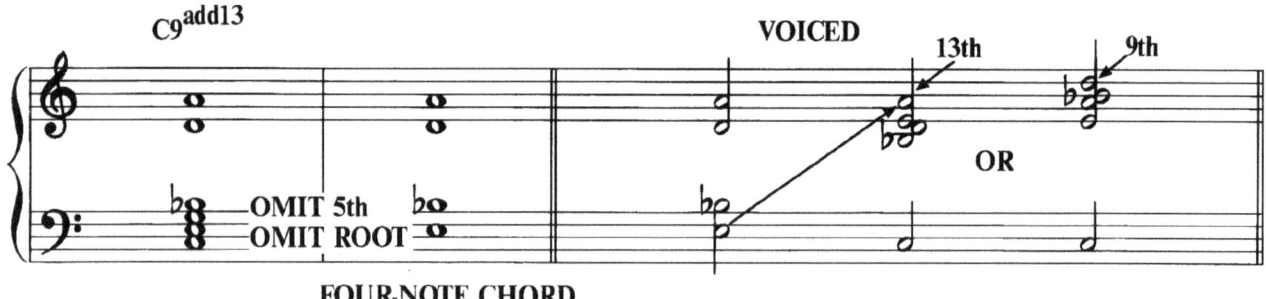

Play the chords mentioned above, on all 12 semitones of the Octave, varying the voicing of each chord.

HANDY MANUSCRIPT

4. GRAPE ESCAPE

This piece is written in the Aeolian Mode on C. It makes use of the Extended chords with added notes in both open and cluster formations.

Exercise. Complete the thirteenth chords on each note of the C Aeolian Mode and then name them.

For further information on the naming of extended chords with altered notes, refer to Book Two of the Contemporary Chord Workbook series by Margaret S. Brandman.

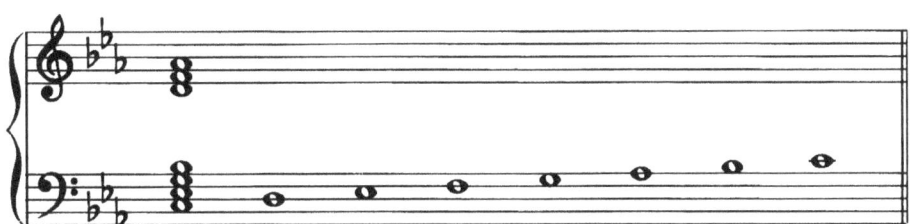

Margaret S. Brandman

ROOT PROGRESSIONS STEP VII
ALTERED CYCLE PROGRESSIONS

The basic Cycle progression can be altered by 'dropping' or 'raising' several of the Root Notes by a SEMITONE.

For example, the usual Cycle progression from E would be: E A D G C F etc. Using the idea of the semitone 'drop' this same progression would use the Root Notes :— E A♭ D♭ G♭ C F. As you can see three of the Root Notes have been altered by a semitone (flattened).

Similarly, an example of a 'raised' progression would be the same Cycle progression beginning on E♭. Thus E♭ A♭ D♭ G C F. In this case the last three Root Notes have been raised a semitone from the Normal Cycle progression.

Practically speaking, each time a 'dropped' Progression is used, a 'raised' progression must be used to bring it back to the original Cycle.

An interesting feature of the altered Cycle progression, is the relationship between the two chords at the point where the altered progression meets up with the original progression. The connection between the Root Notes of the chords, at this point, is the interval of a TRITONE (3 tones distance otherwise known as a Diminished 5th or Augmented 4th interval). In the first of the above progressions, G♭ to C, and in the second progression, from D♭ to G.

The Dominant 7th Flattened 5th chord, can be used on either Root Note (or both) to smooth the transition from section to section. When you work out the notes of the D♭7♭5 and G7♭5 chords, for instance, you will realise that they consist of exactly the same notes. The flattened fifth note in the D♭ chord is A♭♭(G) and the flattened fifth note in the G chord is D♭. The connection between the flattened fifth notes of both chords is also a Tritone.

Thus, the altered cycle progression can be subtly inserted in many cases without disturbing the flow of the progression or in some cases without the listener realising that alterations have actually been made.

Example 1 (a and b) uses these altered progressions in the context of a 12-Bar blues progression. Keep in mind that by using these sounds, you are moving into the realm of Mainstream Jazz sounds and departing substantially from the raw 'Blues' sound. Example 1a presents the basic progression showing the Root Movements and suggesting some chord qualities to use.

Example 1a

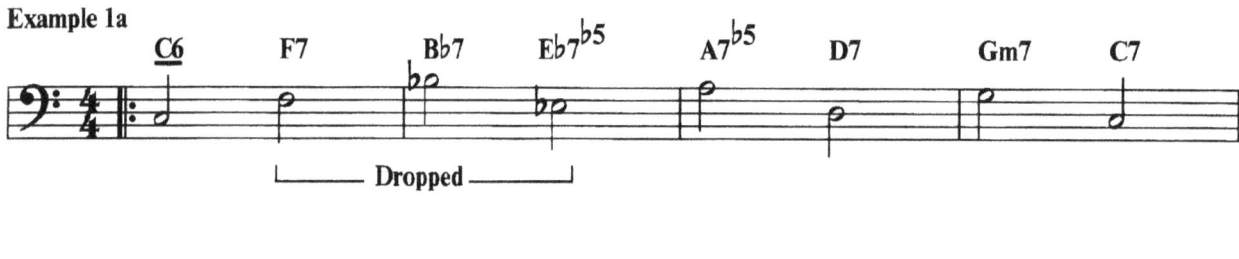

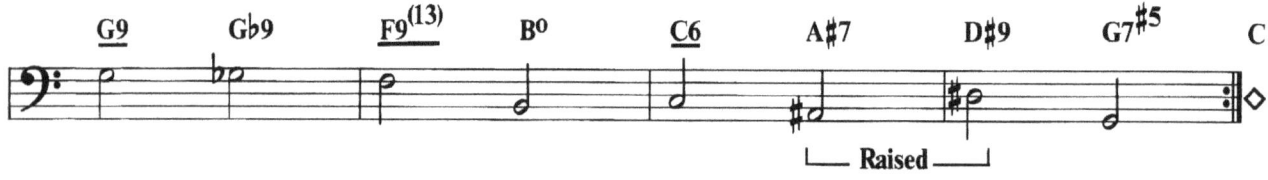

N.B. Those chords that have been underlined are "Goal Chords".

Example 1b, is one treatment of this progression using open chord voicings.
See also the section on voicing in Fourths on page 65.
Play the example first as written and then applying some of the suggested rhythmic figures, as well as some of your own choosing.

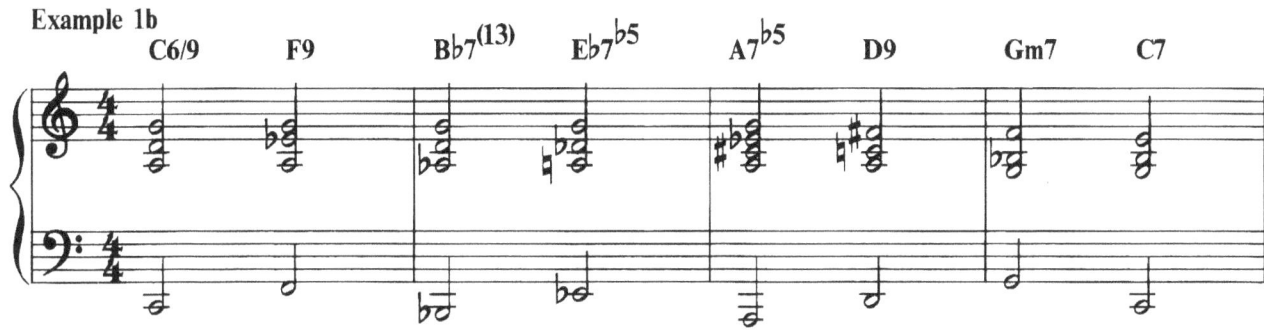

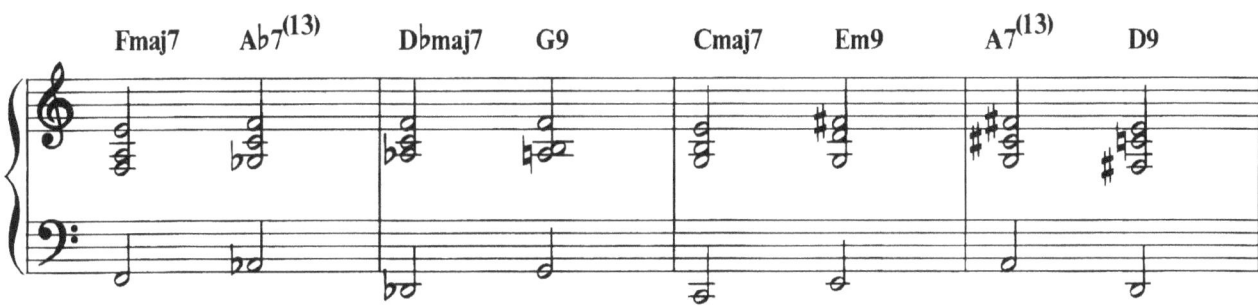

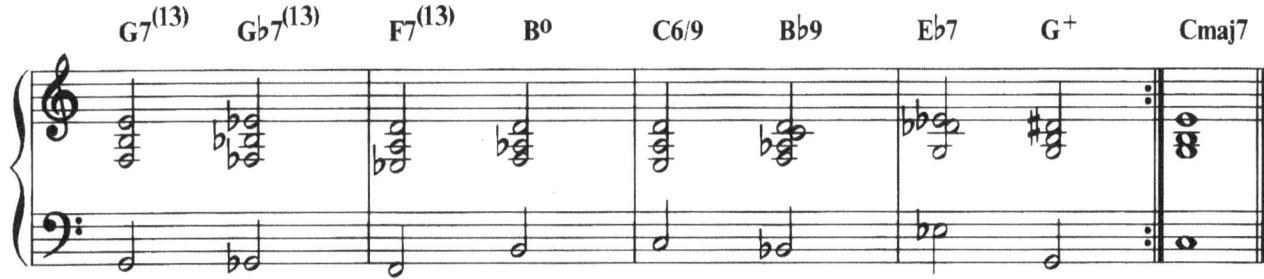

SUGGESTED RHYTHMIC FIGURES

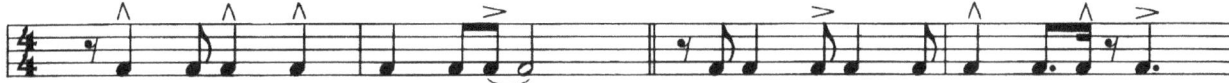

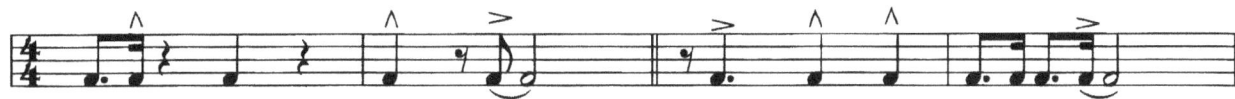

APPLICATION OF STEP VII

The use of the altered Cycle progression will lend an interesting change of colour to many Jazz Tunes and Standards.

When using the chords built on the altered Root Notes as 'Substitute' chords, ensure that the melody note blends with the chord.

This blending can be approached from several different points of view depending on your musical taste and intention.

(1) The melody note may blend perfectly with the altered chord, if it is a common note to both chords. (This will sound correct but the altered chord will lend the tune a more interesting colour).

(2) The melody note may not match the altered chord exactly, in which case the quality of the chord could be changed. For instance, use a Minor 7th chord instead of a Dominant 7th, or Flatten or Sharpen one of the notes within the chord. (i.e. b5, #5, etc.)

(3) The melody note may be discordant with the chord. This effect may be desirable for various musical reasons. Sometimes the discord can be softened a little by altering the supporting notes. This is entirely up to the performer's or composer's taste (and that of your audience!)

ETUDE No. 2

F. Chopin

The following study in 'two against three,'* by Chopin serves as a good example of the types of Root Progressions so far discussed.

Write the chords in above the music and then refer to the next section of text to see how the chord progression can be explained in terms of Root Progressions. The first sixteen bars and the last twenty bars do not differ greatly from the types of progression we have already covered so I have left them to you, the student, to analyse.

From bars 17 to 20 there is an altered cycle progression (Step VII), up a semitone. In bars 21 to 24 there is a modulation to the IIIrd of the key (C Maj) (Step V). The final chord of this section (the G7) provides the link to the next section which is based on a climbing chromatic scale from G up to C (Step III or VII) (Bars 24 to 29), while the next section moves to the key of Ami — how chromatic can you get? — via a ♭V(E♭mi) to ♭II(B♭) to iv (Dmi) to i⁶₄ (Ami) to V(E) to i (Ami) progression. (This progression can also be viewed as an altered cycle progression, moving in 4ths). See Bars 29 to 33.

The following section, bars 34 to 37, moves to the key of B♭major (Chromatic chord II of the original key centre) via the progression minor v (Fmi) to ii (Cmi) to minor iv(E♭mi) to I⁶₄ (B♭) to V7 (F7) to I (B♭).

Next there is a quick Dominant to Tonic movement in Fmi (C7 to Fmi) in bars 38 and 39, then a stepwise descending Root Movement (Step IV) from D♭ to C to E♭/B♭ to A♭ — home key.

The final section is once again solidly based on the home key. Note the use of ninths and elevenths as extension notes to the chords.

The more you investigate the music of Chopin the more you will appreciate how far ahead of his time he was and how harmonically interesting his music can be.

This Urtext version of the piece will need to be played with your own ideas on phrasing, touch, dynamics etc. superimposed onto the original setting. These ideas should be gained by listening to performances of Chopin's music and the music of other composers of the Romantic period.

*Refer to page 167 in Book 2B of this series for information on the manner in which to count 'two against three.'

USE THIS SPACE TO DRAW UP CHORD TABLES FOR THE PIECE.

5. TROIS ETUDES. No. 2

F. Chopin

FIGURED BASS EXERCISES—SECTION 5

Seventh Chords in Second and Third Inversions and the Diminshed Seventh Chord

As mentioned in Book 3 the figuring for the second inversion of the Seventh chord is $^6_3$ which is usually shortened to $^4_3$.

The figuring for the third inversion of the seventh chord is $^6_2$ which is usually shortened to $^4_2$.

One way of remembering these is that they are the opposite of the inversion number, that is — the Second inversion has the number 3 in it while the Third inversion has the number 2 in it.

After completing the Chord Table, write in the chord names above each bar and the degree numbers below each bass note. Then play Exercise 1.

CHORD TABLE

Exercise 1

The Diminished Seventh Chord

As you have seen the Figured Bass system was the short-hand system used in the 16th and 17th centuries. There was even a chord symbol for the Diminished Seventh chord. This symbol is a seven with a line through it — ꝡ, and it is a little larger than the other numbers.

As the chord is not written in full there is no need to specify which inversion has to be used and of course the chord is the same shape as the other three diminished sevenths which use the same notes.

Complete the chord table and then play Exercise 2.

CHORD TABLE

Exercise 2

MUSICAL SOUND SOURCES

4. Harmony

The concept of a strong tonal centre with Dominant-Tonic cadences has largely been abandoned except in popular music.

Some works are written on a system of tonal levels centering on a pedal note in order to provide some cohesion to the ideas.

If works are written in 'Keys' there is usually a large use of Chromatic notes and chords and altered chords. This is particularly true of Jazz compositions.

Bitonality (two keys) and Polytonality (many keys) are other devices that are employed. (See page 80). There are many examples of Bitonality in Bartok's 'Microcosmos' for Piano.

Quartal Harmony (based on 4ths) and Quintal Harmony (based on 5ths) can be found in the music of many 'Serious' composers, notably Debussy, but has found particular favour with the jazz musicians of the West Coast school of thought. (The West Coast of America). Any recent book of Jazz voicing will discuss this subject in detail. (See page 65).

Also refer to Number 8 in my book *Contemporary Modal Pieces*.

BELLS ACROSS THE WATER

The following piece in the Locrian Mode, employs Quartal and Quintal Harmony. The bar lines are used simply to indicate the main accent for a section as there is no Time Signature.

The crotchet (Quarter-Note) is the Beat Note.

If your piano has a Sostenuto pedal (a third middle pedal) use this pedal to sustain the held bass notes while pedalling normally with the sustain pedal for the high chords. (Refer to Book 2, page 56 for more information on the sostenuto pedal).

IMPROVISATION

Experimenting with the Quartal and Quintal harmony, exhibited in Bells Across the Water, choose a Mode in which to improvise your own piece. If you like the piece enough to want to capture it for posterity, write it out and store it in a book of your own original material.

Use the manuscript below to write out your chosen mode and sketch out some ideas for improvisation.

6. BELLS ACROSS THE WATER

Margaret S. Brandman

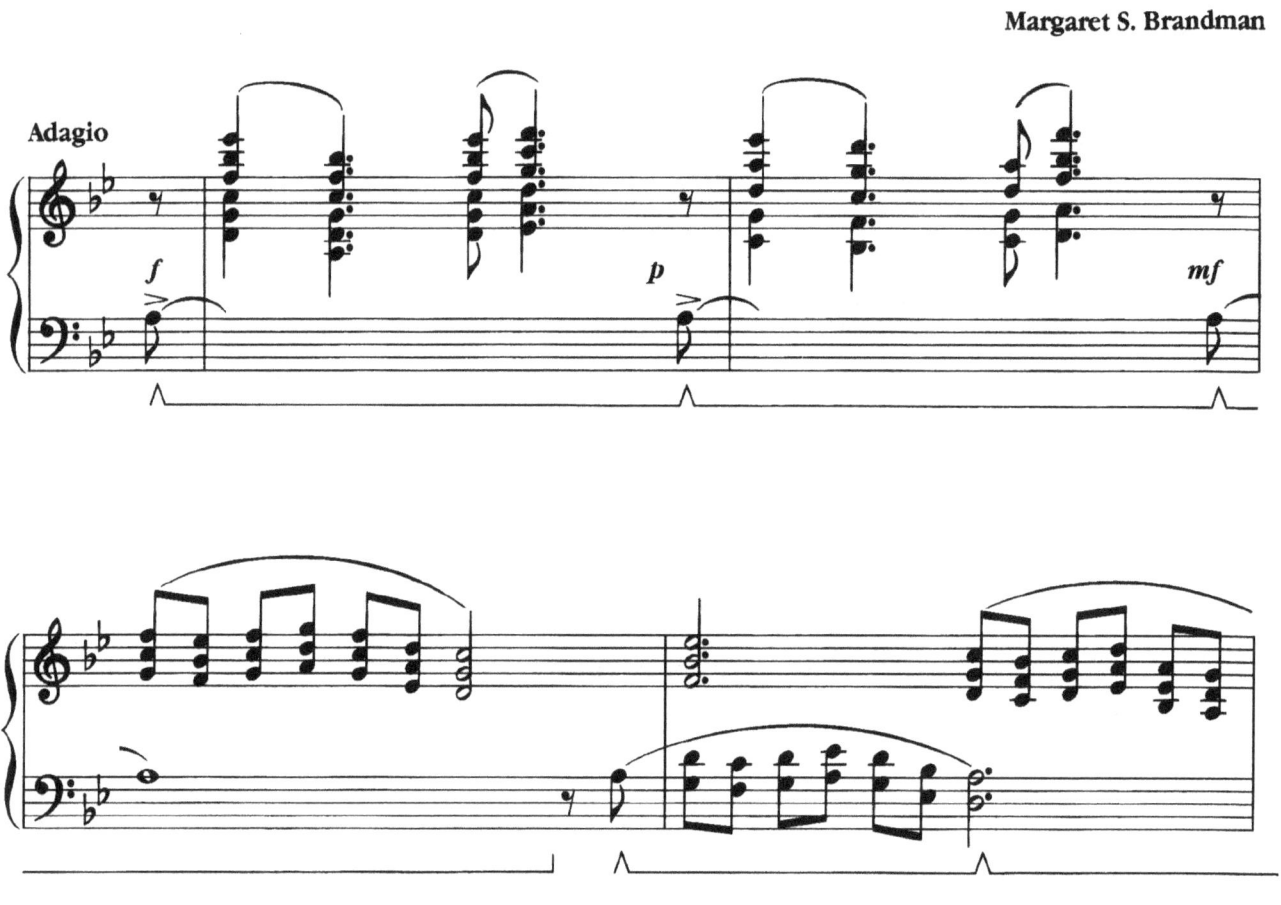
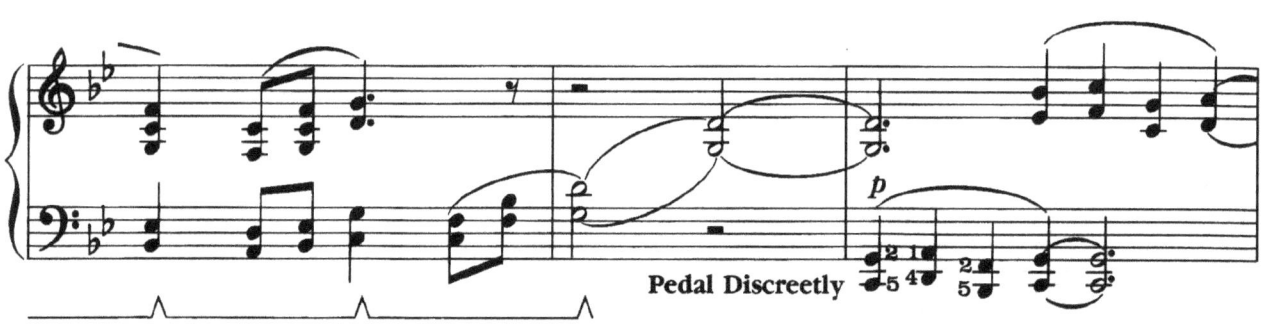

Leave Pedal down until
Harmonics have subsided. ENJOY!

FIGURED BASS EXERCISES—SECTION 6

(a) Using the Suspended Fourth and Suspended Ninth degrees.
(b) Modulation.

(a) The Suspended Fourth chord which uses the 1st, 4th 5th and 8th degrees is indicated by the number 4 which is taken to mean that the fourth degree is used to replace the third degree of the chord.

Similarly, the Suspended Ninth chord which uses the 1st, 3rd, 5th and 9th degrees is indicated by the number 9 which means that the eighth degree is replaced by the ninth.

Below are several voicings of the Suspended 4th and Suspended 9th chords.

Complete the table and then play Exercise 1.

CHORD TABLE

Exercise 1

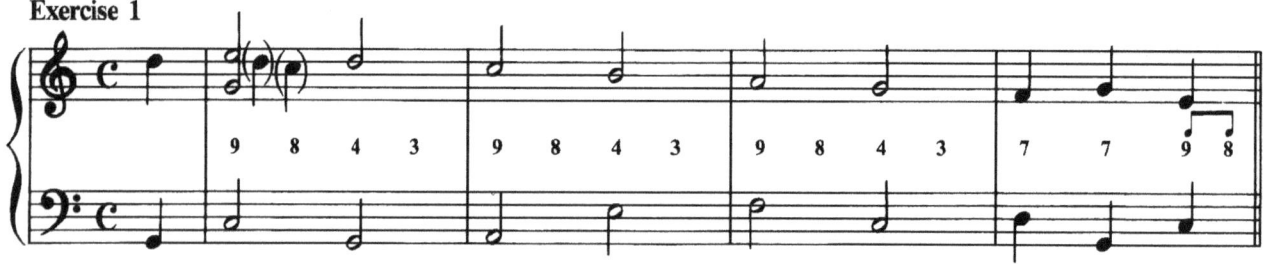

(b) **Modulation**

Modulation is indicated in Figured Bass, as it is in most music by the introduction of accidentals into the music or into the figuring. Often the same note is indicated twice — once by the accidental in the figuring and once by the accidental written before the note in the treble stave. This does not mean repeat the note, but is written this way for the sake of correctness. Only play the affected note once in the chord.

When playing sections which modulate, it is wise to bracket the area and indicate the final cadence. If you have room on the page you should write a Chord Table for each modulatory section.

Complete the Chord Tables, bracket the sections and then play Exercise 2.

THREE-PART INVENTION No. XI

J.S. Bach

The following piece is No. 11 from the 'Three-Part Inventions' by J.S. Bach. The set of 15 pieces is a companion set of pieces to the Two-Part Inventions. Originally, the Three-Part pieces were known as 'Symphonien' from the original meaning of the word 'sounding together'.

The Three-Part Inventions are written in a similar style to the Two-Part pieces, containing the same imitative techniques and devices as were discussed in Book 3 of this series.

This particular example, makes use of some very pleasant cycle progressions and is a good example of how to construct a progression in a minor key.

When analysing the piece, first look for the modulations and while you are playing the piece make sure that your thinking is adjusted to suit the new scale so that your fingers will follow the correct pathway for each key. Indicate the modulations clearly on the music.

In imitative music it is very useful to think 'horizontally' as well as 'vertically' and knowing the scale pathways, is an aid to thinking this way.

Secondly, analyse the chords and progressions (vertical) by writing the chord names above each bar.

A recommended practice procedure for music that is written in three or more voices, is to dissect the parts, playing each one through separately. By doing this you allow the ear to learn what each part sounds like and this will be of great help when you synthesise the parts together. Your ear will more successfully guide you to bring out one part more than another at various points during the performance of the piece so that you are able to present an interesting interpretation of the written notes.

Try to make each statement of the 'Subject' distinct from the other accompanying parts so that the listener can say 'I've heard that before!' As with pop music, it is often not until the second or third hearing that the listener says that he/she likes the tune. So try to make your performance of the piece strike the note in the listener which says — I know that tune, I could sing along with it!

As the Swingle Singers know, Bach wrote some great melodies which are eminently singable. If you capture this idea in your playing you will make his music come alive.

7. THREE-PART INVENTION No. XI

J.S. Bach

35

ROOT PROGRESSIONS STEP VIII
EQUAL DIVISIONS OF THE OCTAVE

Root Progressions moving along equal divisions of the octave, have been a fairly common compositional device since 1940 when the American conductor, theorist and composer Joseph SCHILLINGER published his musical theory in a manual entitled 'Kaleidophone'.

The 'Schillinger System' owes its origin to his training as a mathematician. According to the system there are as many tonics as there are equal splits of the octave. This is a substantial departure from the traditional harmony of the Major/Minor system which revolves around the Cycle of Fifths.

THE SYSTEM:—

As the octave consists of 12 semitones it can obviously be split in several ways:

(a) Into HALVES — 6 semitones from each other. For example the Tonics of C — F sharp — C. The distance between these tonics can also be called an Augmented 4th, Diminished 5th or Tritone.

(b) Into THIRDS — 4 semitones distance from each other. For example the Tonics of C — E — G sharp — C. The distance between these Tonics can also be called a Major Third. The Tonics therefore move along the notes of an Augmented Triad.

(c) Into QUARTERS - 3 semitones from each other. For example the Tonics of C — E flat — F sharp — A — C. The distance between these Tonics can also be called a Minor Third. The Tonics therefore move along the notes of a Diminished Seventh chord.

(d) Into SIXTHS — 2 semitones from each other. For example the Tonics of C — D — E — F sharp — G sharp — A sharp — C. The distance between these Tonics can also be called a Tone. Therefore the Tonics move along the Whole-Tone scale.

(e) Into TWELFTHS — 1 semitone from each other. The Tonics therefore move along the Chromatic scale.

The sounds created by building chords on the above Tonics will obviously be quite different to those sounds of the Cycle of Fifths Root Progressions discussed on the previous pages. The usual use of these Tonics, is to place a Major chord on each one, so that the music seems to move abruptly from key centre to key centre. See Example 1. Play this example and try to recall where you have heard this sound before.

EQUAL DIVISIONS OF THE OCTAVE

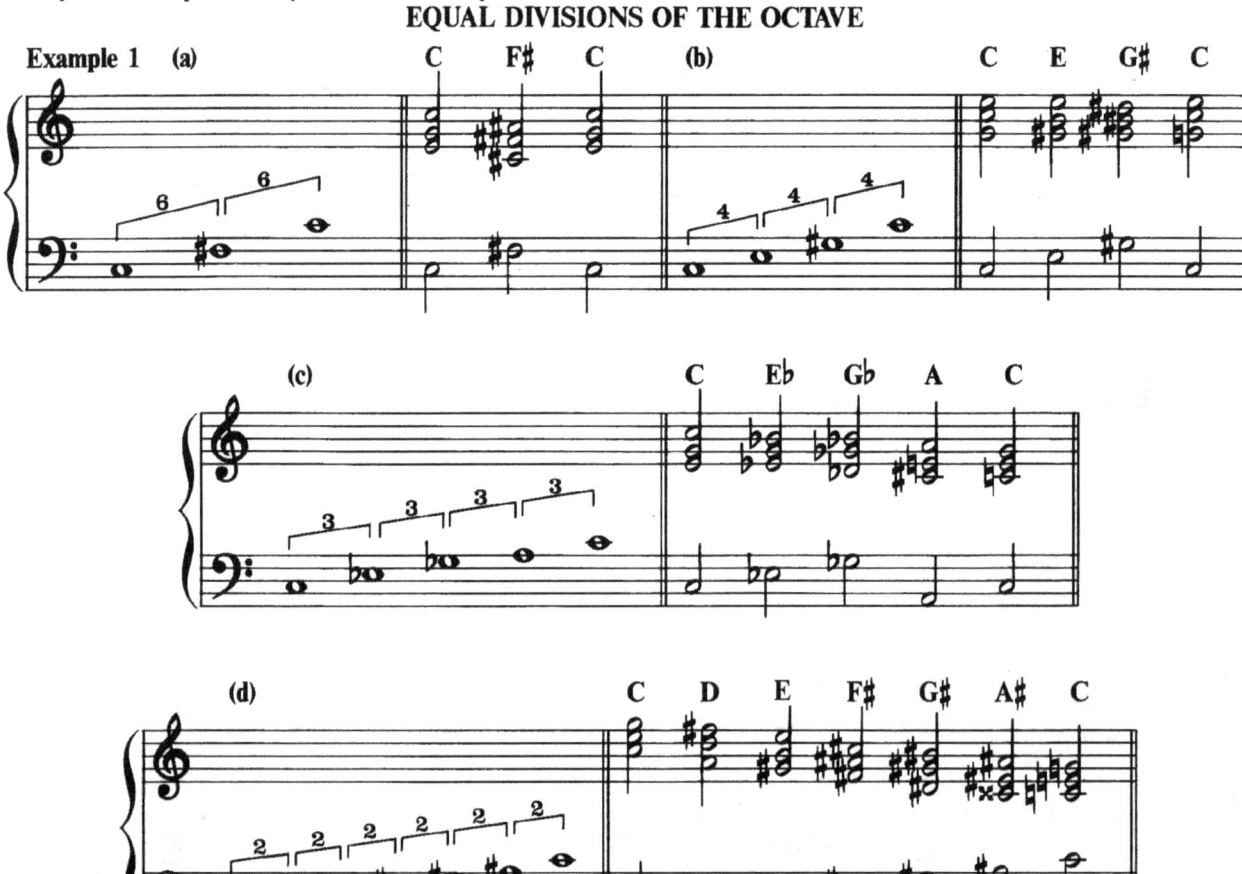

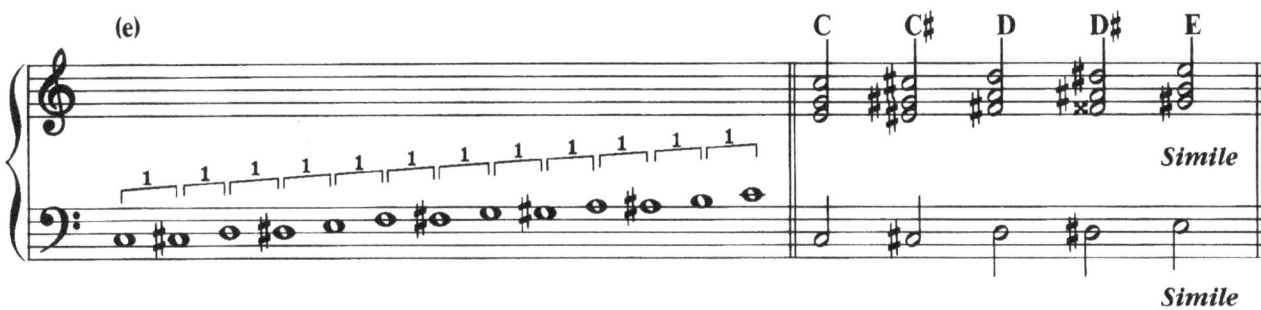

Did the sounds remind you of the movie scores of the 1950's? Movies such as Ben Hur whose score was written by Miklos Rozsa, and all the countless epic dramas and horror movies of the time.

Personally, I believe that, knowingly or not, many of the New Wave and Punk bands are arriving at the same sounds, possibly due to the fact that they know only a limited number of types of chords (Major or Minor etc.) and shift these chords from position to position on the guitar.

Example 2

As these sounds are no longer appropriate in a Blues progression, I have written a chord progression using the Schillinger system. The goal chords are underlined. For the experimental and curious student, the system should provide a good starting point for some interesting compositions, using varying chord qualities above the Root Notes.

The underlined chords are goal chords.

Special Note:

The Tonics moving along the Chromatic scale, have been utilized in Traditional and Jazz Harmony and do not belong exclusively to the Schillinger system.

Refer to Step II Root Progressions — Substitution of the Flattened Second Degree for the Dominant Degree. Also refer to page 46 for some effective Progressions built on the Chromatic Scale.

IMPROVISATION

Using a written chord structure of your own choosing, based on Root Progressions moving along equal divisions of the octave, improvise a short piece. Incorporate some of the ideas you have gleaned from other composers works and music you have recently listened to.

DANSES DE TRAVERS No. 1

by Erik Satie

This piece provides a good example of how far ahead of his time Erik Satie's music really was. Note the free style of composition without bar-lines or Time-Signature.

The Root Movements in this piece include many movements along the Equal divisions of the octave. Analyse the chords and Root Movements before playing the piece.

Be sure to distinguish the upper melody lines from the accompanying arpeggio movement.

8. DANSES DE TRAVERS

MUSICAL SOUND SOURCES (Continued)

5. Rhythm

Rhythm in 20th Century music is treated in a variety of ways in order to achieve freedom from the traditional 4 or 3 beats to the bar or measure. Some of these ways are as follows:

(a) Irregular meters. Refer to Numbers 13, 16 and 19 in Contemporary Modal Pieces and Numbers 1, 7 in Book 3 and Number 15 in this book.

(b) Polyrhythms that is: two or more rhythms moving at the same time.

(c) Displacement of Rhythm, using accents to create a bar within a bar. See the following piece, in the whole-tone scale.

(d) Using a bar line in a random fashion in order to indicate the strong beat of the section. Refer to Numbers 6 and 10 in Contemporary Modal Pieces and number 6 of this book.

(e) Using frequent changes of time signatures within the piece. Refer to numbers 7, 8 and 9 in Contemporary Modal Pieces and numbers 3 and 4 in this book.

(f) Free Time either using a particular note as the beat note with no bar lines, or using new notation to indicate the effects. Often these pieces introduce an element of controlled improvisation where the performer decides the duration of each section. Refer to Numbers 1 and 18 in Contemporary Modal Pieces and numbers 1 and 8 in this book. this book.

(g) Greater use of Syncopation. Refer to Numbers 5 and 17 in Contemporary Modal Pieces.

IMPROVISATION

Improvise a piece in the Pentatonic scale using some of the above rhythmic suggestions.
Use the manuscript below to jot down some ideas on which to base your improvisation.

MUSICAL SOUND SOURCES (Continued)

6. **New Notational Devices**

   Look for many different types of notational devices and the composers instructions as to how to interpret them. A few of these are listed below.

   (a) To continue an arpeggiated section ad lib:

   (b) A free section where the basic beat is approximately a quaver showing which hand plays the notes in sequence:

   (c) The crossed note used to indicate any extra-musical sounds.

   (d) Cluster Notation:

   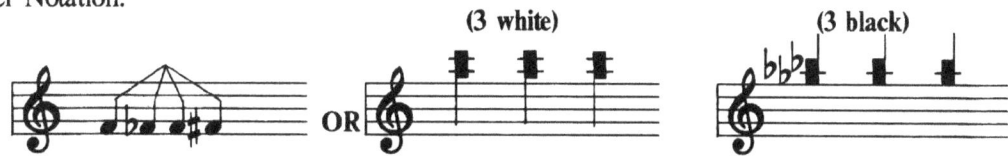

   (e) Larger Cluster to be played with the Flat of the hand:

   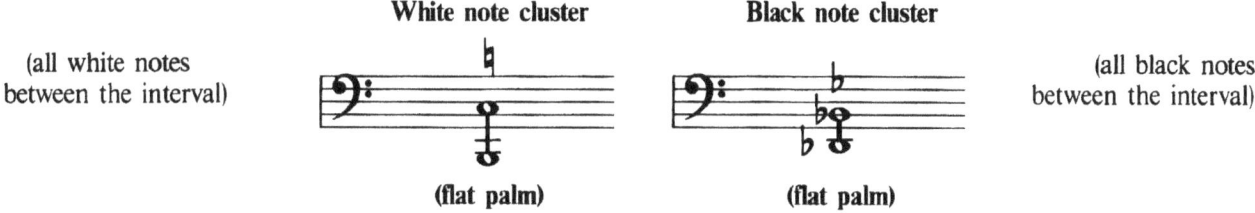

Refer to the following works for examples of Modern Notational Devices.
*Nos 4 and 14 from **Contemporary Modal Pieces**, Sunshowers on the River from **Six Contemporary Pieces**.*
Sonorities (Advanced Piano Solo) and Static Ripples (Piano Duet) all by Margaret Brandman.
*Also No 2 from **More Picture Pieces** for Young Pianists by Dulcie Holland.*

THE WHOLE-TONE SCALE

The Whole-Tone scale is one of the scales created when the octave is divided into equal parts. (Refer to page 36 in this book.)

There are only two forms of the scale as six whole tones only divide twice into the 12 semitones of the octave.

Several composers have used the Whole-Tone scale to colour their music. Among the first of these was Claude Debussy (1862–1918) who used the scale in addition to Eastern scale sounds, for example the Pentatonic scale, to achieve the shimmery sounds attributed to Impressionist music. Refer also to Number 11 in my book Animodes and 'What's around the Corner' in More Picture Pieces by Dulcie Holland.

In Jazz Improvisation the scale can be used over the following chords: Augmented Triad, Dom7♯5 and Dom7♭5, Dom9♯5 and Dom9♭5. It can also be used over a Dominant 7th chord, with the clashing notes providing a 'Blues' effect.

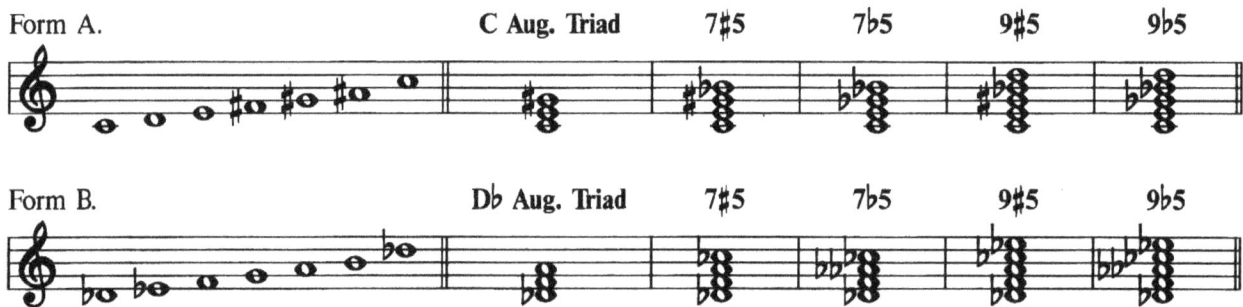

Over a Dominant Seventh Chord.

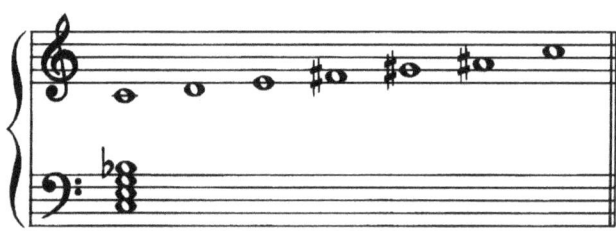

9. WHOLE IN ONE

Margaret S. Brandman

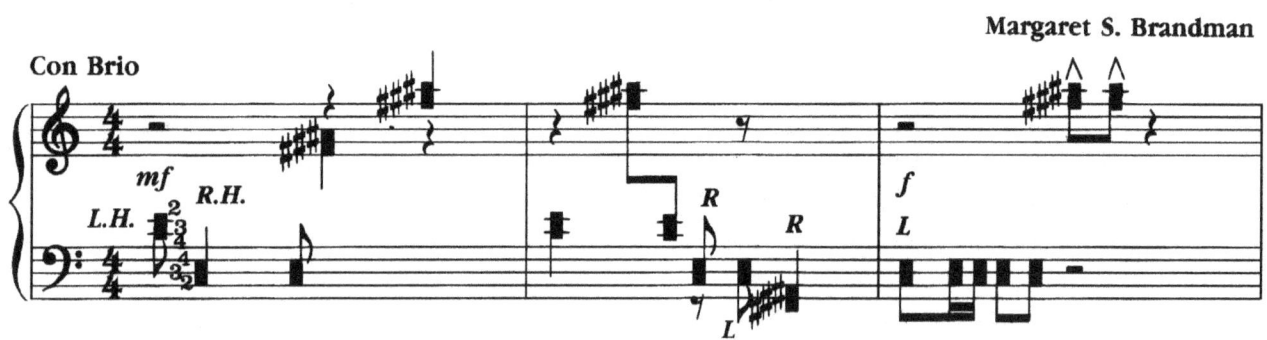

PLAYING TWO-HANDED SCALES AT THE DISTANCE OF A THIRD, SIXTH OR TENTH

A useful technique to develop, at this stage, is the ability to play both Major and Minor scales as well as the Modes, with the hands at either a THIRD, SIXTH or TENTH from each other. Scale passages such as these occur in a great deal of piano music from the Classical Period on and you will save yourself much valuable practice time if you have already mastered the skill.

As an added benefit, playing scales in this form (apart from the pleasant sound and variety they provide) develops co-ordination and evenness of touch as well as confirming the fingering that has been previously applied to the scale.

THIRDS. To play scales in thirds, begin with the Left Hand on the First Degree of the scale and the Right Hand on the Third Degree in close position. For example:

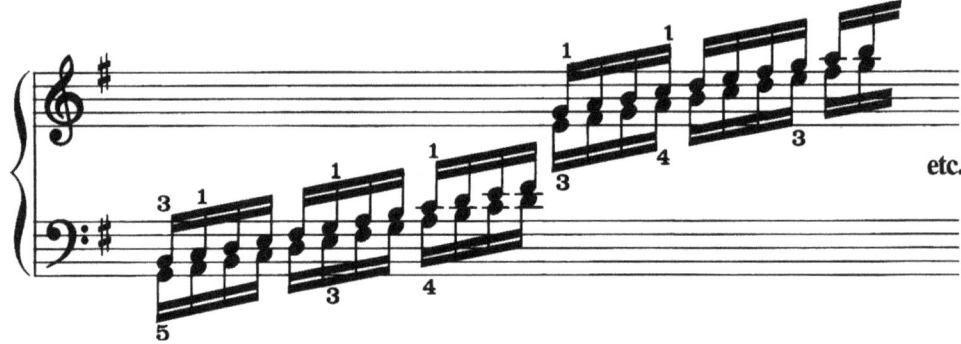

Use the fingering that was originally on the Third degree in the Right Hand and continue as per the original scale. Remember where the fourth finger was placed in the original scale, as it will fall on the same note in this scale form.

In fact the **main clue** for correct fingering of all these scales, is to remember which note is played by the **fourth finger** of each hand.

TENTHS. To play scales in tenths, simply play the right hand an octave higher than the starting note in the thirds.

For Example:

SIXTHS. To play scales in Sixths, invert the starting notes of the scale in Thirds. Take the First Degree with the Right Hand and the Third Degree with the Left Hand. Thus:

For Example:

You will find that in many cases in scales in sixths, the fourth fingers of each hand are depressed at the same time. Play all the scales you have learned in Thirds, Sixths and Tenths.

CHROMATIC PROGRESSIONS

Step VIII in the series on Root Progressions, included a section on Root Movement along the Chromatic scale. Chromatic Progressions can be arrived at from several points of view.

(1) As part of the Schillinger system (refer to page 36).

(2) As part of Traditional Harmony. In the search for more interesting sounds, most of the Romantic Composers (1800 to 1900 approx.) used Chromatic Progressions.

(a) One of these types of progressions was the altered Cycle of Fifth progression where the chord qualities of some of the chords are changed. For instance, instead of moving from chord ii (min) to chord V (dom) to chord I (maj) in a Major key, chord ii was often changed to a Dom 7th, so that the progression moves II (Dom 7) to V (Dom 7) to I (maj). Refer to Step I of the series on Root Progressions.
 In a case like this the movement of an **inner part** follows the Chromatic Scale.

(b) Another of the common Chromatic alterations was to treat Chord IV in a Major key as a Minor Chord. For example a progression such as I V iv I. See Book 2 page 121.

(c) Also Chord V was often altered to an Augmented Chord for a change of colour. See Book 2, page 121.

(d) The other important Chromatic Chord type was the chord built on either the Flattened 6th or Flattened 2nd degree of the scale. (On Flat VI the Italian, German and French 6ths and on Flat II the Neapolitan 6th). Refer to Book 3 (Root movement along the Chromatic Scale).

(3) As part of Jazz Harmony, using the device of the Flattened Second degree as a substitute for the Dominant Seventh Chord. (Refer to Book 3). In this instance, a small section of the Chromatic scale is used. A progression which originally moved ii to V to I would become ii to ♭II to I.

SOME EFFECTIVE CHROMATIC ROOT PROGRESSIONS

Presented below are a few effective usages of extended progressions moving along the Chromatic Scale.

(1) **The Ascending Pattern** (See Example 1)
The first progression is one which moves from I to ♯I to II to ♯II to III using Diminished Seventh Chords on the Chromatic notes. It can also be viewed as an extension of STEP III of the Root Progressions. (Refer to Book 3).

The origin of the Progression would be as a Diatonic progression from I to II to III using the Dominant 7th of each, as a leading chord. Thus in C Major the original progression would be I(C) to II(Dmi) to III(Emi) using A7 to lead to Dmi and B7 to lead to Emi; C A7 Dmi B7 Emi. If the Diminished 7th chord on vii is substituted for each Dominant 7th chord, the progression then becomes I(C) to ♯I(C sharp dim 7th) to II(Dmi) to ♯II(D sharp dim 7th) to III(Emi). As you no doubt realise C sharp dim 7th is the Seventh chord in the key of D minor and likewise, D sharp dim 7th is the Seventh chord in E minor.

However as the progression is moving so quickly from one key to the next it is more convenient to view the whole progression in relation to the starting chord, regarding each alteration as a CHROMATIC chord.
This type of progression of course, can be used as a linking progression between other degrees of the scale.

Example 1

(2) **The Descending Pattern. III—♭III—II—♭II—I** (See Example 2)

The descending pattern is an extended version of Step II in the Root Progressions. The origins of the pattern would once again be in the diatonic pattern of III to II to I using the Dominant Seventh of each as a leading chord. For instance in C Major, III(Emi) to VI(A7) to II(Dmi) to V(G7) to I(C). The result is also a Cycle progression. (Step I).

As each Dominant 7th is replaced by a chord on the Flattened Second degree of the scale, the progression becomes based on the Chromatic Scale.

Thus: III(Emi) to ♭III(E♭mi) to II(Dmi) to ♭II(D♭mi) to I(C).

The progression also works with the following chord qualities:— E7—E♭7—D7—D♭7—C Maj7, or Emi7—E♭mi7—Dmi7—D♭7—C Maj7.

Once again experiment to find which chord qualities suit your purpose.

Example 2

(3) **The Mixed Cycle and Chromatic Pattern. V—I, ♭V—♭I etc.** (See Example 3).

In this pattern the Root Movement is from Dominant to Tonic followed by the Dominant and Tonic of the Key a Semitone Lower. For instance beginning on the note E the progression would move E to A, E♭ to A♭, D to G, D♭ to G♭, C to F, B to E, B♭ to E♭ and so on. Every second chord is a Chromatic note away. Once again the relationship between neighbouring chords is the TRITONE. The progression is subtly different to the Cycle progression, not exactly the same as Step 1, yet not 'way-out' enough to cause consternation.

Example 3

Example 4

This is another Twelve-Bar Blues pattern using the Chromatic patterns mentioned on page 46 as substitute chords. Keep in mind that these patterns can occur in many different styles of music and that in fact many tunes were written with these chord patterns as their basis.

Play these chords first as Sixths and Sevenths and then extend the chord into a Ninth, Eleventh or Thirteenth chord.

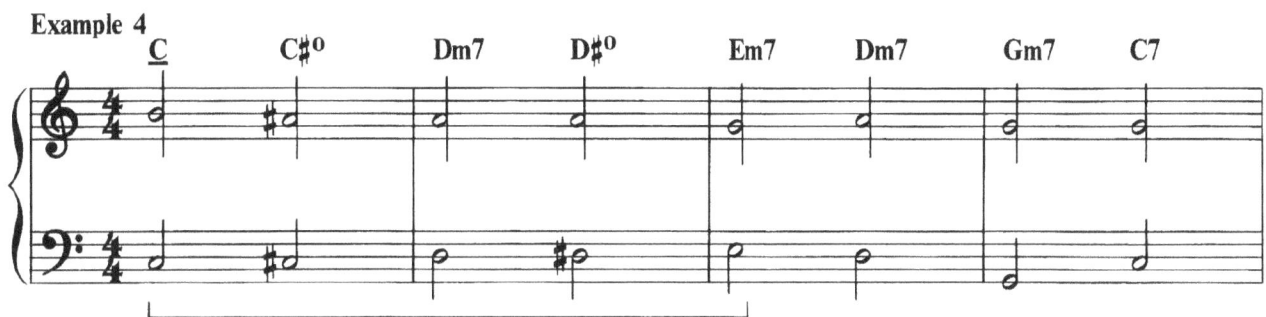

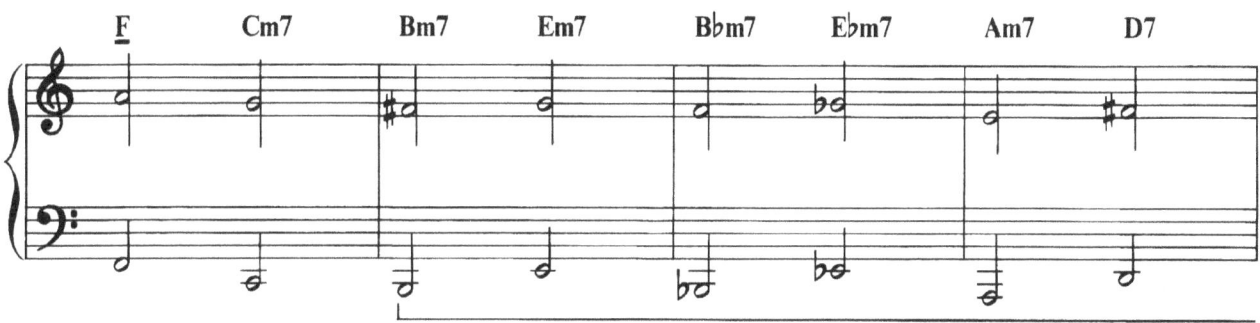

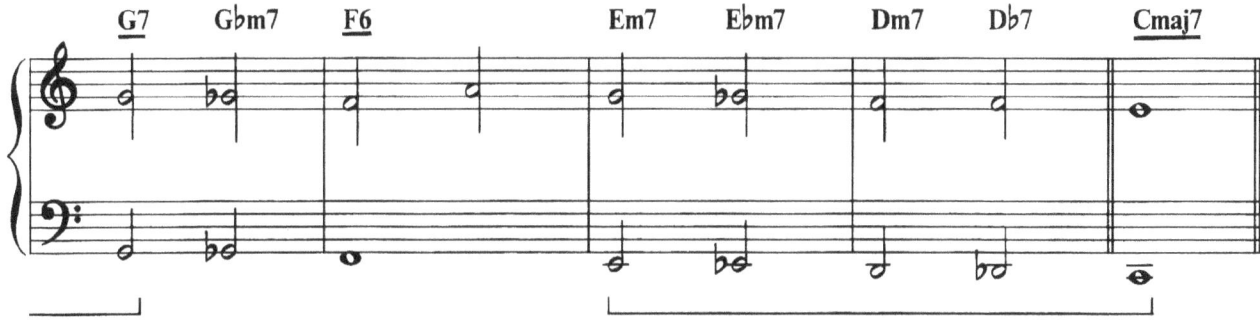

Example 5

This example gives some Jazz 'comping' rhythms to apply to the progression in Example 4.
(a) Right Hand comping figures.
(b) Left Hand comping figures for use with Right Hand Improvised lines.

THE WELL-TEMPERED CLAVIER

This is the name given to the set of 48 Preludes and Fugues by J.S. Bach, which were written to demonstrate the new tuning system which was being adopted at the time, that is Tempered Tuning. (See Book 3, Page 77) for the discussion on Real and Tempered Tuning.

To demonstrate the versatility of the new system Bach wrote a Prelude and Fugue on each note of the Chromatic scale, in both the Tonic Major and the Tonic Minor keys. For example the first Prelude and Fugue is in C Major and the second is in C Minor. Number 3 is in C♯ Major, Number 4 in C♯ Minor, Number 5 in D Major and Number 6 in D Minor and so on. Thus it takes 24 Preludes and Fugues to complete one set. There are therefore two sets of 24 Preludes and Fugues making up the complete Well-Tempered Clavier series. The first set was completed in 1722 when Bach was 38 and the matching set was completed in 1744. A translation of the full title of the work from Bach's own original title for the work is:—

'The Well-tempered Clavier, or preludes and fugues in all the tones and semitones, both with the major third or Ut, Re, Mi and with the minor third of Re, Mi Fa. For the use and practice of young musicians who desire to learn, as well as for those who are already skilled in this study, by way of amusement; made and composed by Johann Sebastian Bach, Kapellmeister for the time being to the Grand Duke of Anhalt-Cothen and director of his chamber music, 1722'.

The Preludes as the name implies are introductory pieces which establish the key and set the stage for the fugue. They are similar in style to the 2 and 3-part Inventions.

There is no better way to get to know one's keys and one's keyboard (clavier) than to play all of the 48 Preludes and Fugues in the set. Once you have played the following example, obtain a copy of Books 1 and 2 of the set and commence learning a Prelude and Fugue every couple of weeks, even if you treat them more as reading exercises than pieces to be performed. If you find one that you particularly favour, bring it up to concert standard while continuing to familiarise yourself with the others in the set.

I would recommend also that the student play some keyboard works of G.F. Handel to find out how this composer employed the contrapuntal devices mentioned earlier, in his Polyphonic compositions.

Use the space below to draw up a Modulation Spider for the Prelude on page 50.
Refer to *Contemporary Piano Method* Book 3 for a Modulation Spider template.

FUGUE

A **FUGUE** (Latin "flight") is a Contrapuntal composition written with two or more 'voices'. The number of voices can vary from 2 to 5. The term 'voice' is used to denote one line be it sung or played.

Each **Subject** is followed by an **Answer** which creates the impression that one part is 'fleeing' or 'in flight' from the other.

Broadly speaking the fugue divides into three sections: the Exposition, the Middle Section and the Closing Section or Coda.

In a four voice Fugue, the **Exposition** begins with the main theme of the Fugue, the **Subject**, being stated unaccompanied in the Tonic key by a single voice. This is then Answered by a second voice in the Dominant key while the first voice continues with complementary material. If this Complementary material occurs in the same form after each statement of the Subject or Answer it is known as a Counter-Subject. If the material is varied or entirely different each time it is simply classed as free material, not Counter-Subject material.

The Answer. If the Answer is an exact transposition of the original Subject, then it is known as a REAL answer and subsequently the whole Fugue is known as a **Real Fugue**. However if the Answer is slightly altered it is known as a TONAL Answer and the Fugue is known as a **Tonal Fugue**.

After the Subject and Answer have appeared in the first two voices there is some bridging material known as an 'Episode'. The episode subsequently leads to the next statement of the Subject and Answer in the two previously unused voices. Once all four voices have alternately stated the Subject and Answer the exposition is complete. This section usually ends with an obvious cadence, usually in the Dominant Key. The Exposition is the only part of the Fugue which follows set rules.

The **Middle Section** is a free section, rather like a Fantasia, which uses all or part of the Subject material as well as free 'Episodic material' moving through many keys and employing many of the Fugal devices. (cf p 37 Book 3).

The **Closing Section** is usually indicated by a return of the Subject in the Tonic key. A feature of the closing section is the use of the Stretto for dramatic effect. Strettos are by no means confined to the Closing section being often found in the Middle section of the Fugue. After the Stretto in the Closing section there is usually some Coda material which brings the Fugue to a close.

Before playing the following Fugue, analyse the modulations and the entries of the Subject and Answer. Write in the necessary information, using S for Subject and A for Answer. When playing the Fugue bring out these themes so that they can be easily recognised by the listener.

Note also the use of the 'Breve' (eight-count note) in the Bass voice in bar 8 and the 'Breve' rests in the opening bars.

Refer to page 141 of Book 2B in this series, for some exercises to develop your part-playing ability.

Use the space below to draw up a Modulation Spider for the Fugue on page 52.
Refer to *Contemporary Piano Method* Book 3 for a Modulation Spider template.

10. PRELUDE IX

J.S. Bach

FUGUE IX

53

THE DIMINISHED SCALE

This is the first of the 'synthetic' scales to be discussed in this book. The scale divides symmetrically into the octave and just as there are only three forms of the diminished seventh chord, there are only three forms of the Diminished Scale.

The basic scale pattern is T S T S T S T S but it can be transmuted to start on the first Semitone. If the same pattern is played on any three neighbouring semitones, or any three neighbouring keys in the Cycle of Fifths, all the forms will be encompassed.

An easy way to view the basic form of the scale is to think of the scale as the **first four notes** of two minor scales (Tetrachords), built on the 1st note and the half-way point of the octave. The result is that the two Tetrachords are linked by a Semitone.

Thus the Diminished scale on C will have these Tetrachords built on C and F♯. The interval is a Tritone which is also known as a Diminished 5th or Augmented 4th.

C DIMINISHED SCALE. (Basic Form Whole-Step, Half-step.)

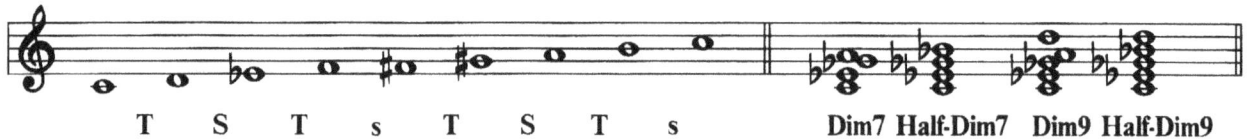

C DIMINISHED SCALE. (Alternate Form Half-Step, Whole-Step.)

In the example above the two forms of the scale and the types of chord over which they can be used, have been presented. Note that in its basic form, the Diminished scale can be used over the half-diminished seventh and ninth chords even though there is some clash between the seventh degree of the chord and the second last note of the scale. (In the example above, the B Flat and the B Natural).

The Diminished scale has been used by several Twentieth century composers. Especially notable amongst these composers is the French composer Olivier Messian who incorporated this scale and other symmetrical scales in his works, regarding these scales as 'Modes of limited transposition'.

Example Two presents the Basic form of the scale on the keys of F, C and G and gives the pattern of black and white notes on the keyboard for these three scale forms.

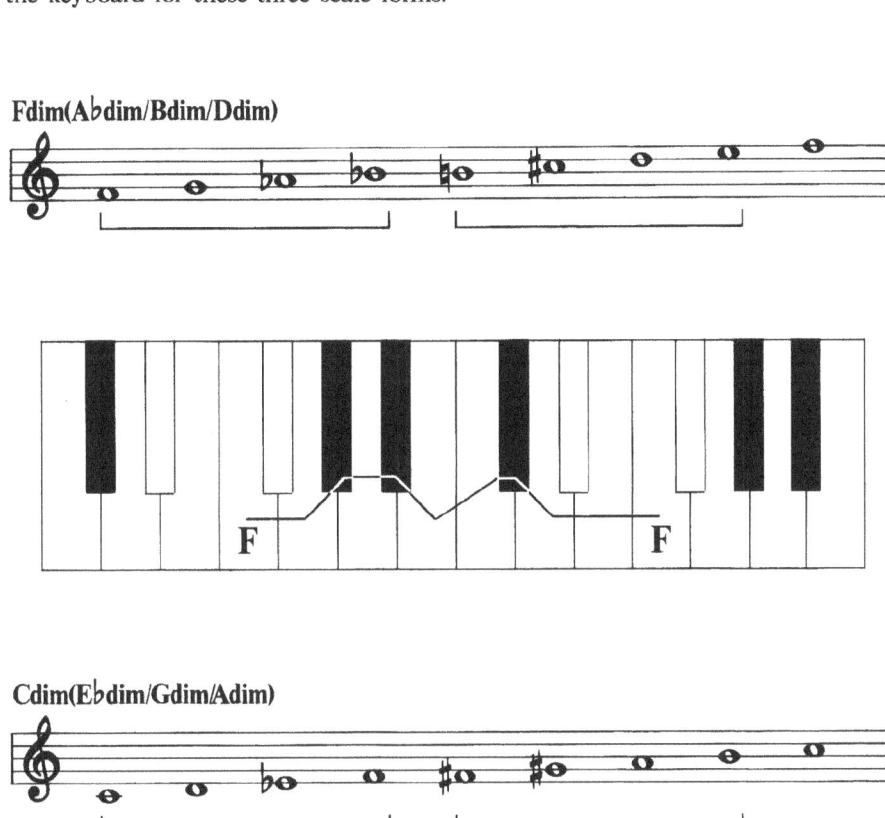

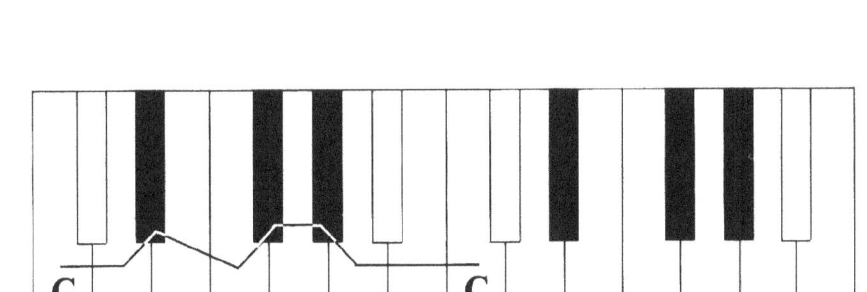

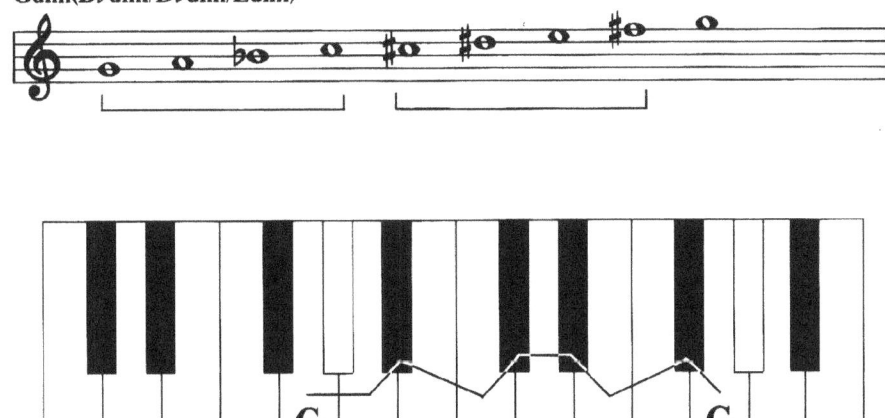

Supply an improvised melody line in the Right Hand above the given chord pattern. Use the appropriate scale or mode for each type of chord. Also given below are some melodic ideas that you can use as patterns for your improvising.

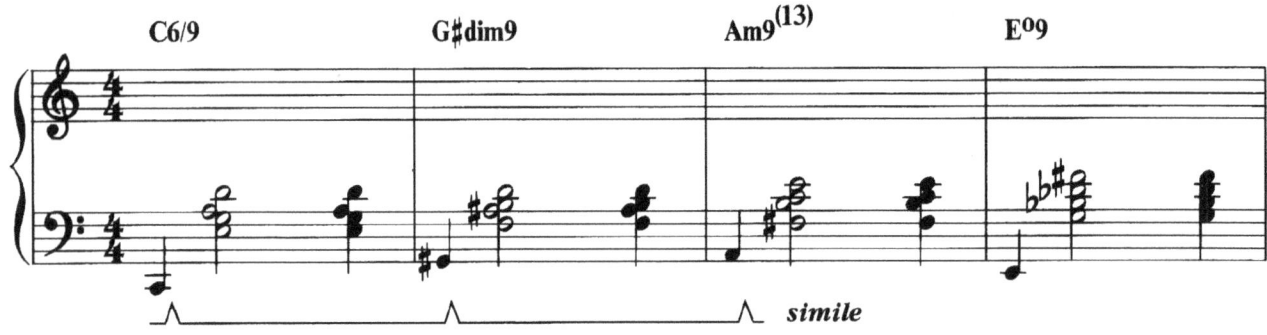

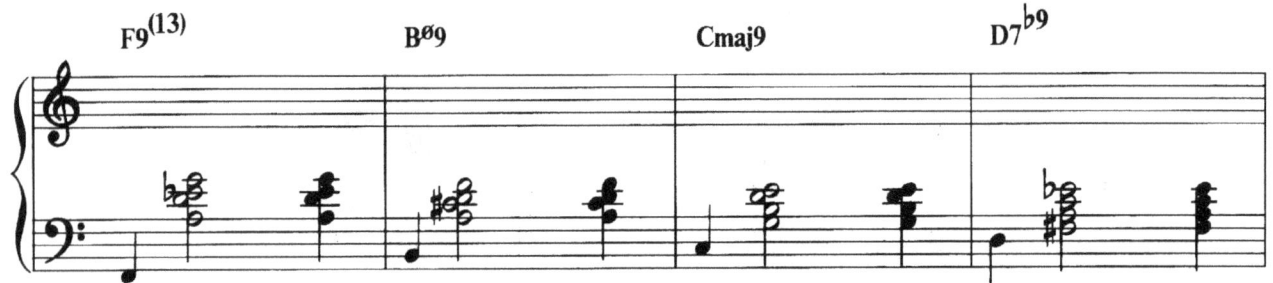

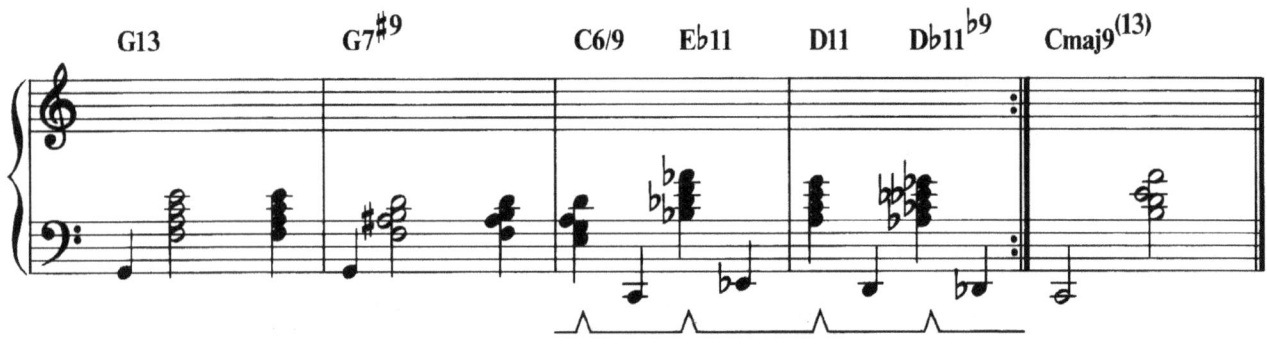

FURTHER TECHNIQUE DEVELOPMENT

If you wish to develop further your technique and fluency, obtain a copy of C.L. HANON's 'The Virtuoso Pianist'.

Work through the exercises in part one of the book, in the written key and also transposed into various major and minor keys. Read the intervals and keep in mind the SCALE PATTERN of the key you are playing. Remember where the groups of **black notes** lie in the keys up to 4 sharps and flats and remember where the **white notes** emerge through the black notes in the keys of 5 and 6 sharps and flats.

In the third section of the book, you will find exercises on Legato Thirds, Double Octave Playing, Sustained Octave playing, trills and tremolos. These are all skills that I would recommend that you develop so that you can call upon them when they appear in the pieces you are reading and learning.

FIGURED BASS—SECTION SEVEN

The following exercise has been written with only the bass line and the figurings. At this stage, you should be able to supply the Right Hand chords without the guidance of the top line for the Right Hand. Use your knowledge of voice leading to ensure that each chord is played in close position to the next and makes melodic sense.

Play the exercise in three different versions beginning each one on a different inversion of the first chord and following on logically from there.

Exercise 1

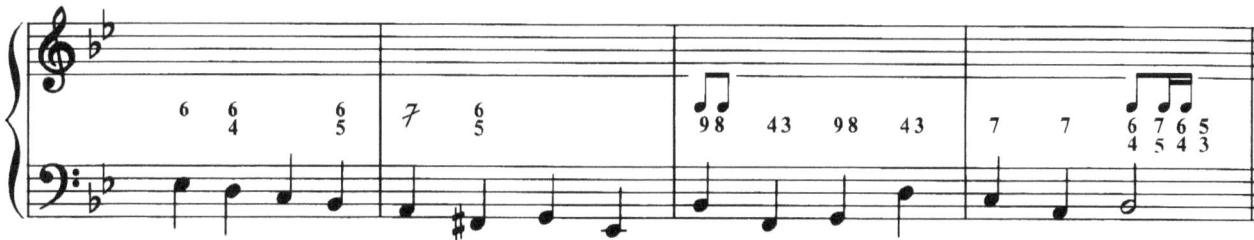

ALTERED NOTES IN THE EXTENDED CHORDS

Section 1.

The following chords can be seen in two ways; (1) as the Altered Seventh chords mentioned previously, used with the addition of one or more of the extended notes (9, 11, 13) or — (2) As the Extended chords mentioned earlier with alterations to one of the four foundation notes.

These chords are:

(1) The Dominant 7♯5 used with the 9th*. e.g. C9♯5.

(2) The Dominant 7♭5 used with the 9th,* or 9th and 11th or 9th and 13th e.g. C9♭5 or C11♭5 or C9(13)♭5.

(3) The Major 7♯5 used with the 9th or 9th and 11th. e.g. CMaj9♯5 or CMaj11♯5.

(4) The Major 7♭5 used with the 9th, or 9th and 13th.* e.g. CMaj9♭5 or CMaj9(13)♭5.

(5) The Minor ♯7 used with the 9th (or 9th and 11th possibly) e.g. Cmi9♯7 or Cmi11♯7.

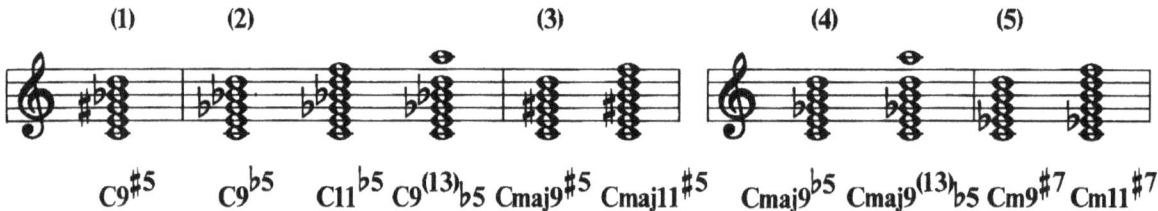

N.B. Those chords marked *, can also be seen as an alternative way of writing alterations to the upper extensions of the chords.

For instance, The Dom 9♯5 is the equivalent chord to the Dom 9(♭13) chord when it is played with its 5th degree omitted. (See page 63).

The Dom9♭5 is the equivalent chord to the Dom9♯11 played with the 5th degree omitted. (See page 63).

The Maj 9(13)♭5 chord is virtually an inversion of the Dominant 9(13) chord a tone higher than the Root note. e.g. CMaj9(13)♭5 = D9(13).

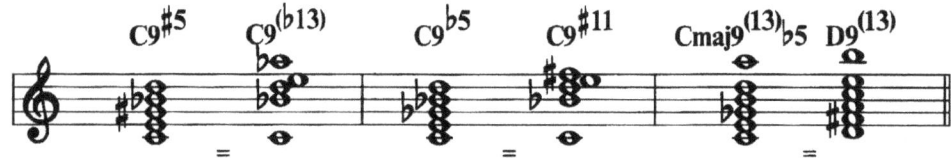

Exercise 1. Find each of the chords mentioned on page 58 in all twelve keys, arranging them for two hands in some of the following styles.

Exercise 2. Play the chord pattern supplying the remaining notes of the chord under the given note. Omit the necessary notes to make the larger chords playable as four-note right-hand chords over the given bass note.

SERIAL MUSIC

The Serial technique of music composition was devised by Arnold Schoenberg (1874-1951) in the early years of the Twentieth Century. Schoenberg began his compositional career in the last few years of the Nineteenth Century writing in the late Romantic style. His work became increasingly chromatic until the stage where Schoenberg decided to abandon tonality altogether. He developed a new method of dealing with the 12 semitones of the octave. The method is known as the Serial Technique or 'Twelve-Tone Technique'.

The essential features of the system are that:
(a) The twelve notes of the octave are selected and arranged to form a twelve-tone 'Row' where each note is used once only until the row is completed.
(b) The Original Row (O) can be used either forwards or backwards (Retrograde -R-) or upside down (where each interval is inverted -I-) or Inverted and backwards (Retrograde Inversion -RI-).
(c) Any form of the row can be transposed to a different pitch.
(d) A note may be repeated only in direct succession, for example

and then cannot be used again until its appearance in the next row.
(e) Traditional melodic treatment (following a natural vocal line) is avoided and the use of wide leaps and angular intervals is preferred.
(f) An accidental applies only to the note directly succeeding it. Therefore Natural signs do not have to be used to cancel a previous accidental and Double Sharps and Double Flats can largely be avoided.

Assignment

(1) Play both numbers 6 and 14 in Animodes* and analyse the use of the Row. Mark the commencement of each Row either O, R, I or RI.
(2) Write your own piece using the given row in all its forms, or a Row of your own choosing, and any other compositional devices (Clusters, Canons, Rhythmic devices etc) that you have learned in this book, on the manuscript provided on the facing page.
(3) Write your title for the piece and your name in the spaces provided.
(4) Play your own piece.

ORIGINAL   **RETROGRADE**

INVERTED   **RETROGRADE INVERSION**

* Contemporary Modal Pieces - formerly Animodes

11.

by ....

ALTERED NOTES IN THE EXTENDED CHORDS

Section 2. Alterations to the Upper extension notes.

The common alterations to the upper extension notes of the chords are as follows: the sharpened or flattened 9th degree, the sharpened 11th degree and the flattened 13th degree. These can be used singly or in combination with each other or with alterations to one of the foundation notes.

The flattened 11th is not used because it is the same sound as the Major 3rd degree, and the sharpened 13th degree is not used, as it is the same sound as the Flattened 7th degree which is already played in the Dominant and Minor 7th chords.)

THE ALTERED NINTH

The Ninth degree can be sharpened or flattened and used either singly or in combination with other altered notes.
Some of the more popular chords using these altered notes are: Dom7♯9 and Dom7♭9 and Dom 13♯9 (played as the 9(13) with the 11th omitted) and the Dom13♭9 chord both with and without the 11th.

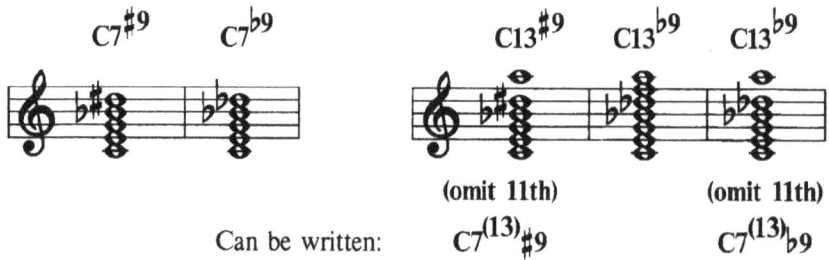

The Dominant Seventh Chord with the Flattened Ninth (minor 9th) degree is the chord that is best suited as the extension chord in a minor key.

Play the following chord progression.

MINOR 7♭9

The Minor 7♭9 chord is in fact the chord named in many traditional harmony books the "Minor 9th" chord. It consists of both a Minor 7th chord and a Minor 9th interval. It is not, however, a very effective Jazz chord and therefore is not in frequent use.

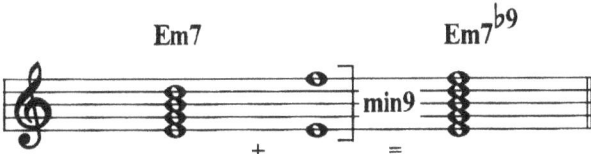

N.B. In some traditional harmony books, the Dominant 7♭9 is also named as a Minor 9th chord. Take care to distinguish between these chords when you come across them in various situations.

THE ALTERED ELEVENTH

The Sharpened Eleventh degree is a very important part of many extended chords. As seen in Book 3 the problem with the Major 13th chord is the clash of sound set up by the use of both the 3rd and the 11th degrees in the same chord. This problem can be resolved by using the Sharpened 11th degree in the Major 13th chord. By using the ♯11 note a smoother blend of sound is created.

The reason for the blend is firstly that the interval of a Minor Ninth between the 3rd and 11th degree is eliminated and secondly that in the Overtone series or Harmonic series the 11th Harmonic is in fact closer in sound to the ♯11 degree than to the Perfect 11th. (See Book 3 for the Harmonic series).

In the Dominant 13th chord this same clash of sound can be resolved by using the Sharpened 11th degree instead of the Perfect 11th. Otherwise the problem is usually solved, as mentioned in Book 3 by omitting the 3rd degree when the Perfect 11th is present. Thus the two types of Dominant 13th chord in common usage are Dom 13 ♯11 (for most Jazz tunes) and the Dom 13 (3rd degree omitted) for Rock and Gospel tunes.

These are the popular chords which use the ♯11:—

(1) Maj9♯11   (2) Maj13♯11   (3) Dom9♯11   (4) Dom13♯11

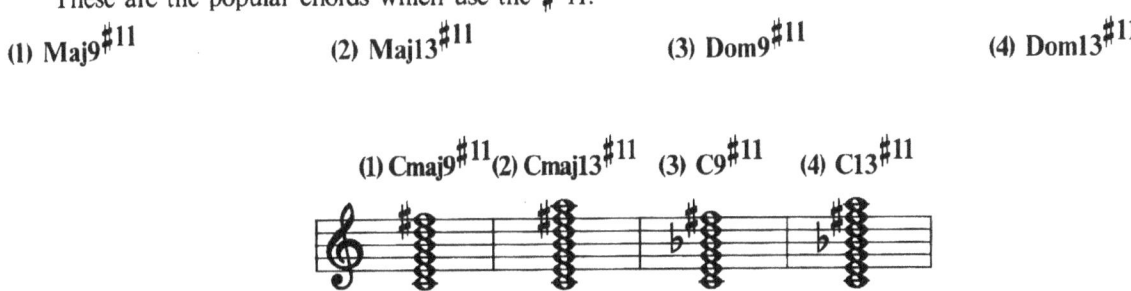

Numbers 1 and 2 can be taken from the Lydian Scale and Numbers 3 and 4 can be taken from the Lydian ♭7 scale. (See page 78).

THE ALTERED THIRTEENTH

The Flattened 13th degree is usually only added to a Dominant 9th or 11th chord. The sound of the chord, when the 5th is omitted, is virtually the same as the Dominant 9♯5 chord.

How the chord is perceived depends largely on the voicing. i.e. whether the altered note is placed in the body of the chord or as the top note.

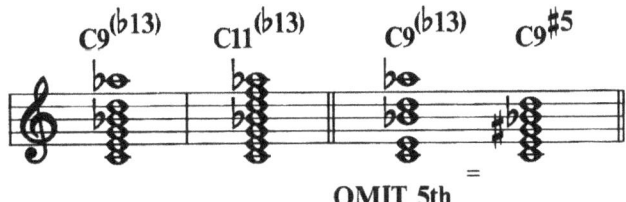

Exercise 1. Play the Altered Eleventh and Altered Thirteenth chords mentioned on page 63, in some of the styles suggested on page 59. Transpose them to all twelve keys.

Exercise 2. Play the following chord progression.

Exercise 3. Play the progression a second time, opening up the voicings by taking either the seventh degree or the fifth degree in the Left Hand and the remaining notes in the Right Hand, as shown in the example.

VOICING CHORDS IN FOURTHS
(Quartal Harmony)

As mentioned earlier in this book, in section 4 of Musical Sound Sources (page 29) Quartal Harmony is greatly favoured by many Jazz musicians.

Most of the extended chords mentioned in Books 3 and 4 of this series, apart from those chords which are constructed symmetrically, can be arranged in fourths rather than in thirds.

For instance, C6/9 can be written either in close position, or with the notes arranged in fourths.

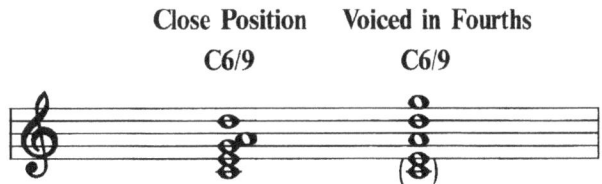

Similarly, C9(13) can be written in close or open position.

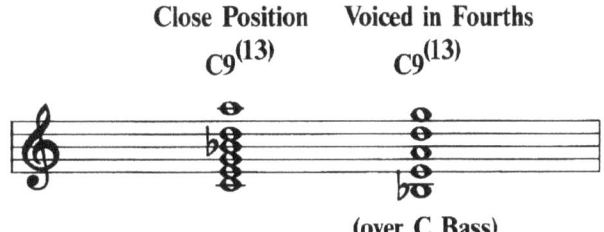

(over C Bass)

SUGGESTED TWO-HANDED VOICINGS

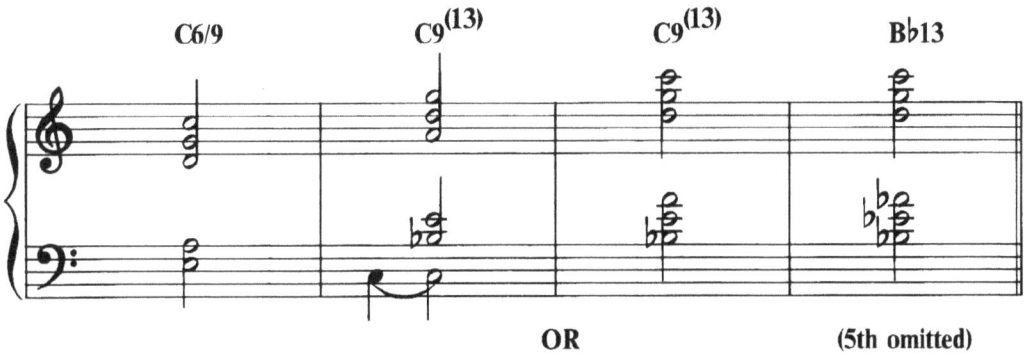

Another common chord that is voiced in Fourths is the Dominant 7♯9 chord. (5th omitted). This is a very versatile chord shape, as it can become a Dom 7(13) (5th omitted) on the degree a Flattened Fifth lower, by simply changing the Root Note.

By altering the Root Note once again, the chord can be transformed into a minor 6/9 chord (5th omitted) or Dim9 (5th omitted) chord of the degree a Flattened Second higher.

Thus the same chords can be used in a progression that moves:

OR

The chord shape is also handy for moving around the cycle of fifths or using the Flattened second as a substitute chord. Play the following chord progressions and note that each note in the chord moves by a falling semitone.

Many of the notes in the chord pattern above are written enharmonically to make reading easy. Keep in mind however, that the shape in the hand is always the same.

Play the following chord progression supplying the remaining notes voiced in fourths (as a three-note right hand shape) below the given notes. Omit those notes which do not fall into the 'fourth' pattern, or cannot be placed into the reach of your hand.

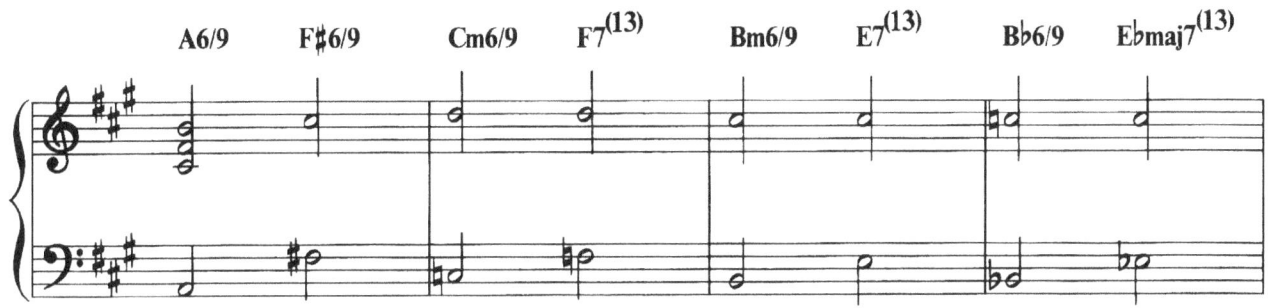

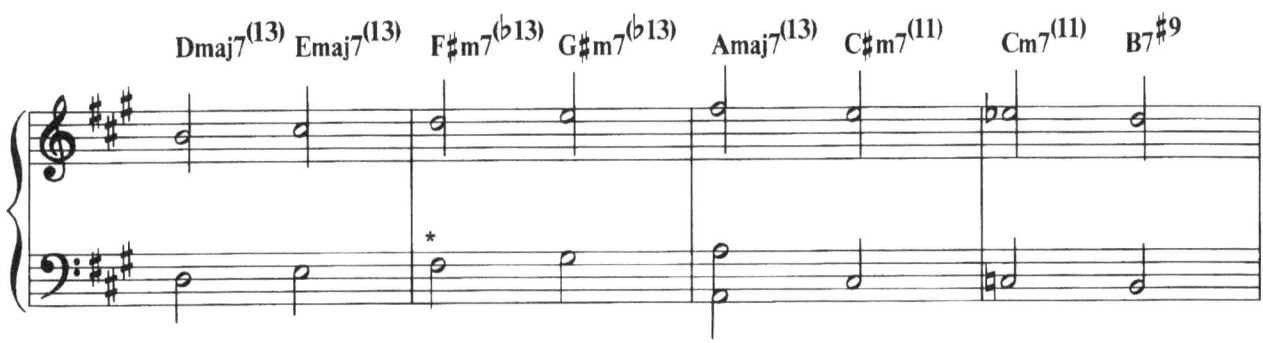

*This chord can also be viewed as an inversion of the D(add 9) chord.

68

The following piece is an arrangement of the Australian traditional song 'Waltzing Matilda' in rather a different style to the usual treatment of the song.

The Quartal harmony which accompanies the melody, lends a rather ambiguous feeling to the tonality. As well, the Root Movement in the B section is by descending whole-tones so that the resulting sound is a combination of Whole-Tone and Quartal Harmony sounds. The Middle section uses an ostinato figure on an F6/9 pedal. The chords in this section can be thought of as Polychords (one chord superimposed over another) or as chords with extension notes. Write the chords in before playing the song.

12. WALTZING MATILDA

Arranged by Margaret S. Brandman.

ALTERED NOTES IN COMBINATION

The following chords are some of the more common usages of altered notes in combination.

(1) Dominant family (a) Dom7♯9♯5   same sounds as Dom7(♭13)♯9 with 5th omitted.
                      (b) Dom7♯9♭5   same sound as Dom7♯11♯9 with 5th omitted.
                      (c) Dom7♭9♯5   same sound as Dom7(♭13)♭9 with 5th omitted.
                      (d) Dom7♭9♭5   same sound as Dom7♯11♭9 with 5th omitted.

(2) Major Family   (a) Maj7♯9♯5   (possible but not highly recommended)

(3) Minor Family   (a) Min7♭9♭5   (possible but not highly recommended)

*OMIT 5th

Exercise. Play the chords above, in all twelve keys. Experiment with different arrangements of each chord as you have done with the previous chords.

Some of the more adventurous combinations, for example a Dom chord with ♯5, ♯9 and ♭9, would indicate a chord which is to be voiced in *FOURTHS. e.g. C7♯9♭9♯5 can be written:

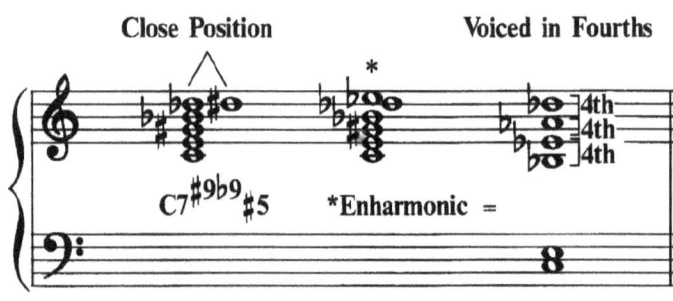

*Fourths — see page 65.

13. *PANCHROMATIC PONDERINGS
Altered Chord Progression

Before playing the following chord study, write the chord names **above** each chord and analyse the progression that is used, by writing the degree numbers **under** each chord. (below the bass clef).

Hint: there is a key change every two bars.

As you play through the progression listen carefully for the sound that the altered notes create. Play SLOWLY so that you can hear all the intricacies. The ear needs time to absorb the sound, and progressions such as this one will only sound jumbled if played too fast.

*Panchromaticism — The compositional use of any or all of the 12 Chromatic notes of the scale, which has the effect of disrupting the sense of key or mode.

FIRST STAR AT TWILIGHT

Chord Types

This piece makes use of many of the Altered Extended Chords discussed on the previous pages in this book. After you have written in the name of each chord analyse the Root Progressions used, using your knowledge of the STEPS in the ROOT PROGRESSION series studied in Books Three and Four of this Method.

As the piece uses numerous chromatic chords, you will find that I have used quite a few 'safety accidentals' so that my intentions are clear. (A safety accidental is one that is used after a bar line even though the bar line cancels the previous accidental. Sometimes they also occur in the middle of the bar to confirm that a repeated note is in fact a sharp or flat, even though technically speaking the original accidental should carry through till the end of the bar.)

Examples of the types of chords you may find in this piece are:
BAR 4   D♭7♯11♭9 and D♭maj13♯9 (no 11th, no 3rd)

Swing Feel

The feel of the piece is a 'Swing Jazz' feel. In general each pair of eighth notes should be interpreted with a triplet feel.

For Example: ♪♪ = ♩♪ and ♪♪♪ = ♩♪♪ and ♪♪ ꜌ = ♩♪ ꜌ ꜌
                1 + a   1 + a   1 + a — played on the first eighth note.

The exceptions are (a) when I have written two Tenuto signs over the eighth notes thus: ♩̄ ♩̄

(b) where the instruction 'Straight 8' is written at the beginning of a section. In these cases play the notes strictly as written.

Any sections in which groups of four sixteenth notes occur must also be played as written, as these groups of four sixteenth notes cannot be 'swung'.

Style

First Star at Twilight demonstrates the sounds and styles of some of the more recent Jazz and Fusion composers and artists. The piece works equally well on both Acoustic and Electric Piano. The Altered Extended Chords have a special richness on Electric Piano.

For further listening in this field I recommend the music of the following artists and composers.
Piano: Bill Evans, Keith Jarret, Chick Corea, Richie Bierach, Ralph Towner, Steve Kuhn, Rainer Brüninghaus and Lyle Mays.
Guitar: Pat Metheny and Jim Hall
Vibraphone: Gary Burton
Bass: Eberhard Weber

Form

The form of this piece is extended Rondo Form. Look for the sections A B A C A B Coda. For more information on Rondo form refer to Book Three in this series.

14. FIRST STAR AT TWILIGHT

Margaret S. Brandman

77

COMMONLY USED JAZZ SCALES

The following scales are often used by Jazz players to improvise over extended chords with and without alterations.

There are many other possibilities available to the creative player including the Ethnic scales listed on page 82. Many scales which do not belong to a specific category can be created by taking various permutations of notes in between the notes of any chord.

For instance the notes of C Major 7th chord could be linked by any or all of the in between notes. Between C and E either C♯, D or D♯ could be used; between E and G either F, or F♯ could be used and between G and B either G♯, A or B♭ could be used. The following scale is just one possibility. See how many interesting variations you can find.

Example 1.

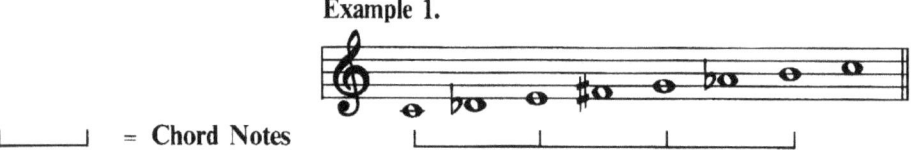

└────┘ = Chord Notes

Jazz Scales

See the facing page for the written scales and chords which they suit.

(1) The Augmented Scale. This is another of the symmetrical scales. Its construction is T½ S T½ S T½ S.

(2) The Blues Scale. Refer also to Book Two in this series. Page 81.

(3) The Ascending Melodic Minor Scale.

(4) The Lydian Augmented Scale. (Lydian Scale with a Sharpened 5th).

(5) The Lydian Flattened 7th Scale. Also known as the Mixolydian Scale with a Sharpened 4th, or scale of the Harmonic Series.

(6) Locrian Sharpened 2nd Scale. This scale is usually chosen in preference to the Locrian Mode as it can be used for the Half-Diminished Ninth chord as well as the Half-Diminished 7th chord.

(7) The Locrian Scale with a Flattened 4th, also known as the Super-Locrian scale, Altered Dominant Scale, Diminished whole-tone scale and Ravel scale. This scale is suitable for all of the Dominant family with altered notes.

Use the manuscript below to write out the Jazz Scales on various starting notes.

Play the above scales on all Twelve semitones of the octave and use them to improvise a melody line on the Root Progression sequences given earlier in this book.

POLYTONALITY AND POLYCHORDS

The terms 'Polytonality' and 'Polychord' both include the prefix 'poly' meaning 'many'. **Polytonality** therefore means having more than one key centre or tonality, while a **Polychord** is one that is built of two or more separate chords.

POLYTONAL MUSIC

The following piece is an example of Polytonal music, as it has the Treble part written in E Major while the Bass part is written in D Major. Many of the pieces in the work 'Microcosmos' by Bela Bartok explore this compositional genre. A favourite pianistic Polytonal device is to place the fingers of one hand along a five-finger position in the key of F Sharp Major (mostly black notes), while the other hand maintains a five-finger position in the key of C Major (all white notes).

Orchestrally, this device could be further explored by placing each group of instruments in a different tonality.

If you analyse the piece you wish to play and discover that it is written in a Polytonal fashion, simply place the fingers along the keyboard patterns for the respective Tonalities and continue to read by intervals.

POLYCHORDS

As mentioned above, a Polychord is one that is built of two or more separate chords stacked above one another. Often the chord will be written in this manner for ease of reading, particularly when many altered notes are involved. For instance $C7\sharp11\flat9$ could just as easily be indicated by $\frac{F\sharp}{C}$, that is F Sharp Major triad over C Major triad.

Some publications use the system whereby the two chords are written directly above one another with a dividing line as is done here, while others use the same system as is used for indicating a chord over a specific bass note; i.e. dividing the two chord names with a diagonal slash.

Refer also to pages 52 and 53 in the Contemporary Chord Workbook, Book 2.

Below are a few examples of Polychords. As you can see, in most cases it is easier to think of these chords as Polychords than it is to try to name them above the Root notes, especially when the chords contain more than seven notes.

FOR EXAMPLE

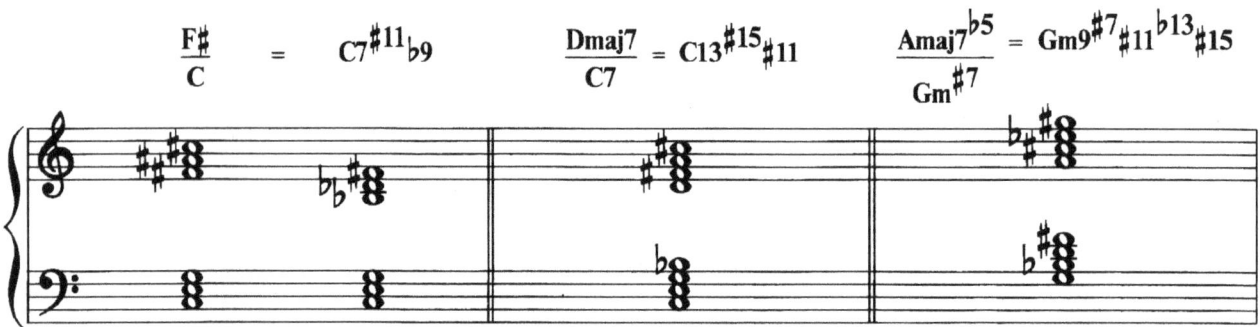

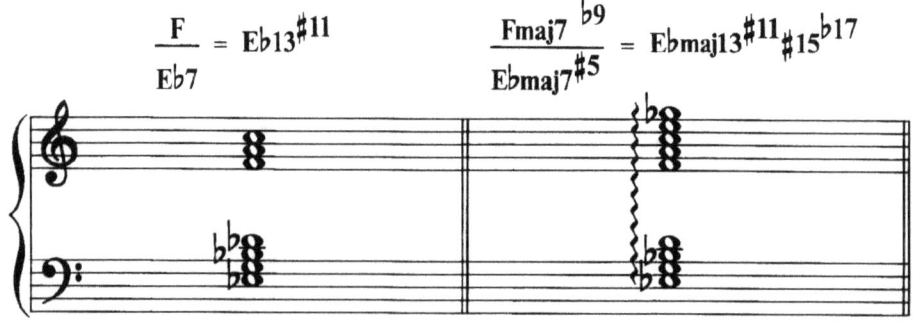

Ped.

15. POLYNESIAN POLYPUS

Margaret S. Brandman

SCALES OUTSIDE THE EUROPEAN CLASSICAL TRADITION

In the latter part of the Nineteenth Century, composers began to think in a more Nationalistic way. This coincided with the political and social developments of the time. Each European country consolidated its territory, either by nationalist wars or by alliances with the smaller states which had previously been autonomous.

Composers reflected this movement by drawing inspiration from their native folk melodies and scales rather than following the Classical Major-Minor tradition.

As communications and travel improved it was also possible to find and use new scale sounds from distant countries. As a result many of the sounds of the Far East found their way into the music of European composers.

With the increased interest this century in 'world music' many composers have already, and will in the future 'borrow' sounds from various cultures, in the quest for interesting means to express themselves.

The scales on the facing page represent just a few of the possible sounds. There are of course many other possibilities when quarter-tones and micro-tones are introduced to the musical language.

For a piece written in the Japanese scale (No. 4) refer to Badinarie Number 1 in Six Contemporary Piano Pieces by the author.

ASSIGNMENT: Improvise a short piece on each one of the scales on the facing page.

A Whole World of Sound

The last piece in this book, uses some of the scales listed below and on the facing page superimposed over each other. You will notice that the Pentatonic scales have been used in the Treble part while some of the other scales provide the Left Hand accompaniment.

The piece has been written in three clefs, a device that is often used so that the implied parts can be easily seen and clearly written. The sustain pedal will have to be used carefully in order to connect the parts but take care not to blur the sound.

If you are playing on a piano which has a Sostenuto Pedal (a third middle pedal which sustains selected notes only), depress this pedal with the Left Foot in order to sustain the long notes on the lowest staff, while pedalling normally with the Right Foot on the sustain pedal for the notes on the upper two staves.

Refer also to the section on Pedalling on page 56 in Book 2 of this series.

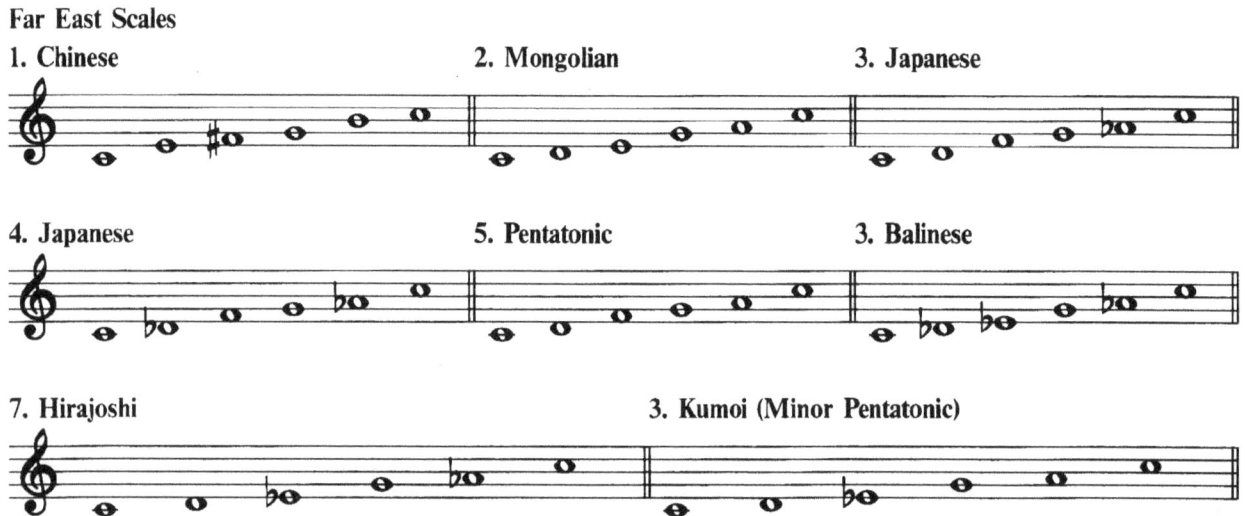

Indian
1. Todi That
2. Purvi That
3. Marwa That

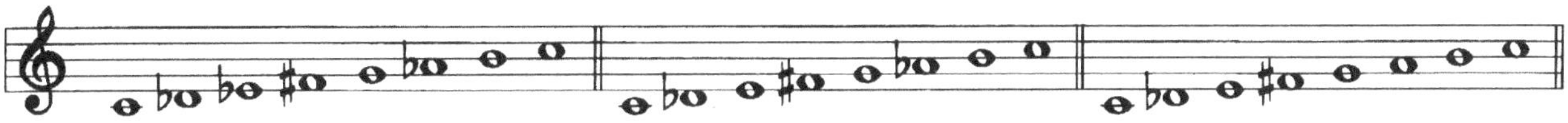

Middle Eastern Scales
1. Algerian
2. Persian 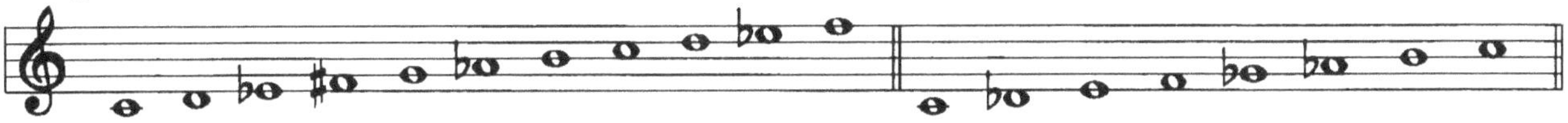
3. Egyptian
4. Arabian
5. Arabian

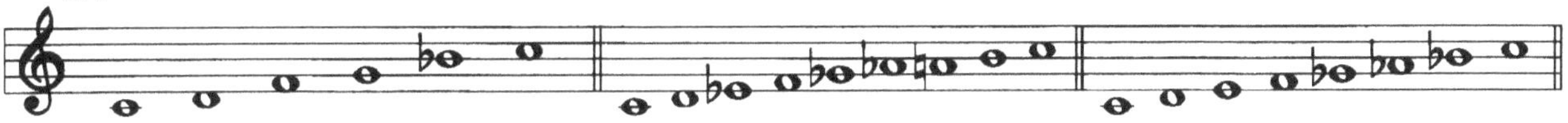

East European Scales
1. Hungarian
2. Hungarian Gypsy
3. Hungarian

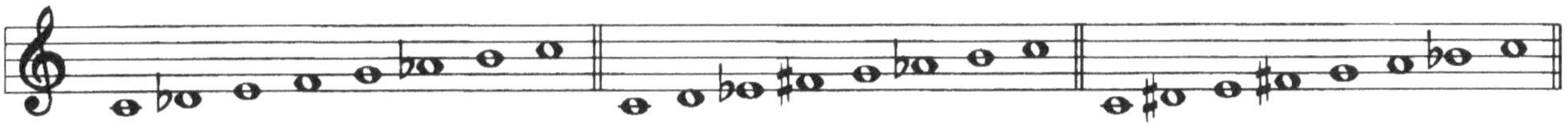

European
1. Neapolitan
2. Spanish Gypsy

16. A WHOLE WORLD OF SOUND

Andante

Margaret S. Brandman

84

www.ingramcontent.com/pod-product-compliance
Lightning Source LLC
Chambersburg PA
CBHW081358160426
43192CB00013B/2438